Joan Fisher's Guide to
Embroidery

Ward Lock Ltd, London

Guide to
Embroidery

by Joan Fisher

ISBN 0 7063 1472 7
Published by
Ward Lock Limited
Designed and produced by
Trewin Copplestone Publishing Ltd, London
© Trewin Copplestone Publishing Ltd 1973
Printed in Spain by
Printer Industria Gráfica sa, Tuset 19
Barcelona, San Vicente dels Hort's 1973
Depósito legal B. 35499-1973
Mohn Gordon Ltd., London

Contents

Introduction

Embroidery, in simple terms, means merely the addition of ornament to a plain fabric. So a flimsy pocket handkerchief with a buttonhole stitch edging is an embroidery; so too is a dramatic abstract wall hanging intricately embellished with surface stitchery, beads, pebbles and bits of ironmongery! Between these two extremes is a vast range of design possibilities, both practical and decorative, traditional and modern.

For a modest outlay, you can buy a few coloured threads, a needle and a piece of fabric, and immediately set to work, to experiment with stitches and techniques, and find out which type of embroidery will suit you: the mathematical precision of counted-thread work where stitches and designs are determined by the mesh of the fabric itself; the diversity of free embroidery where almost anything is possible, from lifelike needlework 'paintings' to classic monograms and initials; the timelessness of canvas work where wonderful rich colour effects are possible, beautiful traditional patterns worked entirely in tent stitch, and modern designs combining literally dozens of different stitches in the one piece of work.

The stitch usually but not always is the means of adding ornament to a fabric; sometimes it is the fabric itself which forms the focal point. In patchwork and appliqué, for instance, a design is created from the fabric shapes and their particular arrangement; the stitching has only a utilitarian purpose in holding the shapes together. In quilting, plain stitching is used in such a way as to create decorative shapes on the padded fabric.

In this book I introduce you to all these different facets of the fascinating and age-old craft of embroidery. Each chapter is devoted to a different 'branch' of embroidery, and gives clear instructions for the stitches and techniques related to that particular subject, plus a number of attractive designs to make up. These designs demonstrate how the stitches and techniques can be used to best advantage, not only in traditional arrangements but in modern applications too.

Embroidery is one of the oldest known crafts – it was one of the earliest methods of painting, of reproducing natural objects in their natural colours – but it is as much in keeping with today's fast-moving mode of living as it was to the more leisurely life-style of our predecessors. In fact, the scope of embroidery has never been wider than it is today: the introduction in recent years of many new fibres and fabrics has opened up a whole new world of design possibilities, and creative ideas . . . all waiting to be captured with needle and thread.

JOAN FISHER

Chapter one
FREE EMBROIDERY

This is probably the most popular 'class' of embroidery work. Each of the specialised branches of decorative needlework has, as you will see in the following chapters, a distinctive and beautiful character, but if we talk about embroidery in general terms, it is undoubtedly free embroidery to which we refer.

There is a tremendous scope for expression in design in this work – a child will find pleasure in working a simple outline embroidery in stem stitch; an experienced embroiderer will be challenged to produce a mammoth and intricate wall hanging with an abstract design; yet another may prefer to depict a pictorial subject, painstakingly and laboriously picking out every detail in a different stitch and colour. All are free embroideries worked on plain backgrounds, the stitches being used to form any shape or size or area as wished.

If you make a mistake in a free-embroidery design, you are not restricted by the limitations of the fabric, or even usually by a particular tradition or technique – turn your mistake to good effect by adding a few extra decorative stitches, being careful of course to keep them in harmony with the rest of the design – and probably no one will ever know!

The following list of equipment, tools and materials applies to free embroidery, and to most other forms of embroidery as well – where specific materials or equipment are required for a different technique these are described in the appropriate chapter.

EQUIPMENT
Needles

The ideal needle for embroidery work should pierce the fabric easily and make a large enough hole for the thread to pull through the fabric smoothly. The thread should also move through the eye of the needle freely. Never use a crooked needle for this will make a crooked stitch.

Sharps are ordinary sewing needles which are used in embroidery with mercerised cotton thread or a single strand of stranded cotton.

Crewel needles are long and sharp and have large eyes. They are used with most embroidery threads – stranded cotton, *coton à broder,* pearl cotton No. 5 and No. 8. Choose a size with a large eye, such as No. 5, when working with six strands of stranded cotton or with pearl cotton No. 5.

Chenille needles are also sharp and have large eyes, but they are slightly shorter then crewel needles. Use the No. 19 size with soft embroidery thread or tapestry wool.

Tapestry needles are used for canvas work and also for counted-thread embroidery on coarse fabrics. A tapestry needle has a blunt end and so is useful for lacing or whipping stitches, too.

Threads

Stranded cotton. This is a shiny, twisted thread. It has six strands which can be untwisted so as many or as few as liked can be used, depending on the embroidery being worked. It is suitable for most types of embroidery.

Pearl cotton is available in two thicknesses, No. 5 and No. 8. It is a smooth, corded thread used for all types of embroidery, but most often for counted-thread work.

Coton à broder is a very twisted, shiny thread, suitable for drawn-thread and drawn-fabric work and cutwork.

Soft embroidery thread is a thick, matt cotton used in most types of embroidery.

Tapestry wool is firm, twisted, woollen yarn, which can be used in ordinary embroidery as well as canvas work.

All these threads are available in a good range of colours. In addition you may find it useful to have basting cotton, a range of mercerised cotton, some metal threads – gold and silver – in different thicknesses and to collect odds and ends of knitting yarns.

If you will want to wash your embroidery a lot, it is best to match yarn and fabric – cotton yarn on cotton fabric, for instance, and make sure your thread is colour fast. Always cut embroidery threads – never break them. Do not use too long a length at a time as it may fray. If it is a twisted thread, make sure it remains twisted during work.

Fabrics

Almost any fabric can be embroidered, but the stitches and design should be chosen to suit the material. Do not waste your efforts on embroidering a cheap fabric which will not last long. For counted-thread work a fabric with an even weave must be used. Evenweave linen is inexpensive and is a very good choice for beginners, too, for either free-style or counted-thread work, as regular stitches can be made easily, right from the start.

Frames

All large embroideries should be worked in a frame, and so should most small ones, particularly if a delicate fabric is being used or if there are areas with a lot of stitches. There are two basic types of frame: the Swiss, or tambour, frame and the slate frame. The tambour frame consists of two hoops, one slightly larger than the other. The fabric is placed over the smaller hoop, then the larger hoop is placed over the fabric so that it holds it taut. Some of these frames have a screw for tightening the outer hoop and some have a stand or clamp so the frame can be placed on a table. If a very fine fabric is being used, it is a good idea to have a piece of muslin or tissue between hoop and fabric.

The slate frame is rectangular and consists of two parallel horizontal bars. Each bar has a length of tape nailed along it. The fabric to be embroidered is sewn to the tape. The side pieces are then slotted into the bars and secured so that they hold the fabric taut. The fabric is laced to these side pieces with strong thread; if a very fine fabric is used, the sides of the fabric should first have strips of tape sewn to them and then the tape is laced to the side pieces of the frame.

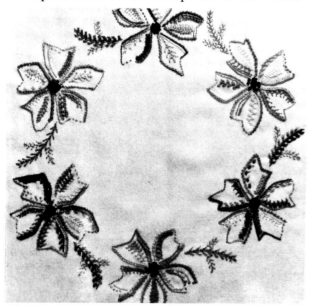

Floral motifs worked on a flannel ground.

Thimble

A metal one is preferable.

Scissors

You will need a large pair for cutting fabrics and a small pointed pair for cutting thread.

Also useful

In addition pins and pounce are needed for transferring designs (see below), a clean white cloth is needed for wrapping the embroidery in while it is not being worked, an iron, ironing board and pressing cloth will be required for pressing the work and a sewing machine is useful for finishing off a piece or making it up into its finished form.

TRANSFERRING
Purchased transfers

There are two types of embroidery transfers – single impression which are used once only, and multi-print which can be used up to eight times: the thinner the fabric the more often can the transfer be used. Cut any lettering away from the transfer and keep aside. Heat iron to fairly hot (wool) temperature for a single impression transfer or hot (cotton) temperature for a multi-print transfer. On a spare piece of fabric test the heat of the iron by placing the cut-away lettering face downwards on the fabric, running the iron over it for a few seconds, then peeling off the transfer. If a good impression has been obtained, place the main transfer in position on the fabric and secure with pins. Apply iron for a few seconds, then lift the corner of the design to make sure the design has transferred properly. If it has not, iron over it again. Make sure you do not move either the transfer or the fabric or the impression will smudge. If on testing the lettering a good impression is not obtained, set the iron a little hotter.

Pouncing

Pricking and pouncing is the traditional method of putting a design on to fabric, and usually considered to be the best one. Trace the design you wish to use on to tracing paper and place tracing paper on a thickly folded piece of spare material. With a needle, prick holes at $\frac{1}{2}$ in. intervals all along lines of design. Place pricked tracing over fabric to be used for embroidery, and hold in place with weights – make sure it is not in a draught. Take a small, tightly-rolled piece of fabric – about the size of a finger – and dip it in pounce (powdered charcoal) for a light-coloured fabric or powdered chalk for a dark one.

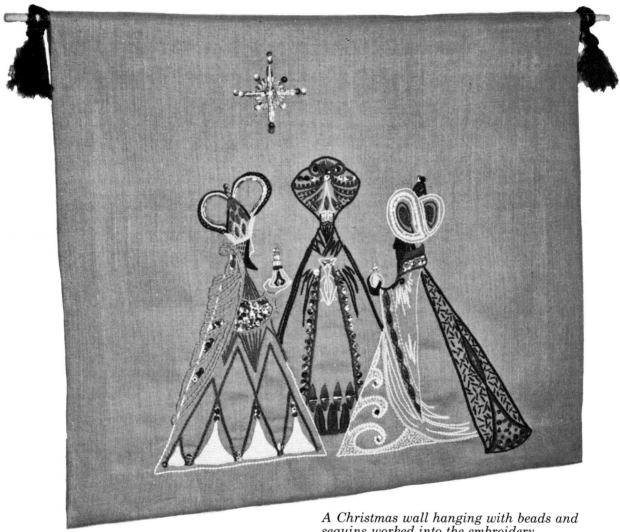

A Christmas wall hanging with beads and sequins worked into the embroidery.

Dab rolled fabric over holes so a little pounce or chalk falls through each hole on to fabric. When whole design has been worked over, remove tracing paper and go over lines with a very fine paint brush and water-colour paint or waterproof Indian ink.

Tracing

A design can be traced direct on to transparent material. Use a fine paint brush and water-colour paint or waterproof Indian ink.

Basting

If a very thick material is being used, the basting method is more satisfactory than the prick and pounce method. Trace design on to tracing paper then place tracing paper over fabric to be used; pin in place. Using a basting thread to contrast with fabric colour, work small running stitches over all the lines of the design through paper and fabric. When complete, carefully tear away tracing paper. Remove basting stitches as soon as possible when working the design.

STITCHES

Back stitch

Work from right to left. Bring thread through on stitch line a little to left of the point where you wish stitching to begin. Take a small stitch backwards, bringing needle out again the same distance ahead of the starting point. This stitch can be laced, if wished.

Blanket and buttonhole stitches

These stitches are worked in a similar way, but blanket (diagram 1) has open stitches while in buttonhole (diagram 2) they are closed. Work from left to right. Bring needle through on lower line, insert at upper line and, holding thread down with left thumb, take a straight downward stitch over thread.

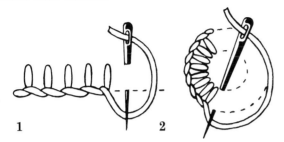

Bullion knot

Bring needle through at left side of point where bullion knot is to appear, then take a small stitch back to the right bringing needle through again at starting point, but without pulling it fully through fabric. Twist thread round needle point as many times as required for length of stitch (about eight times gives a satisfactory stitch) and hold coil with left thumb. Pull needle through. Take it back to the right again, insert and pull fairly tightly so knot lies flat.

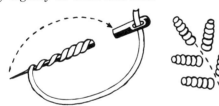

Cable stitch

This stitch is worked from left to right. Bring the needle through on the line of the design, and insert a little to the right on the line, and bring out to the left at the midway point of the stitch, with the thread below the needle (diagram 1). Work the next stitch in a similar way but with the thread above the needle (diagram 2). Continue in this way, alternating the position of the thread. This stitch may also be worked in counted-thread embroidery on an evenweave fabric.

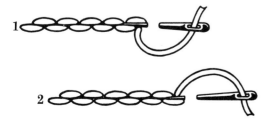

Chain stitch

Bring thread out at top of stitch line, make a loop and hold down with left thumb. Insert needle at starting point again and bring out a short distance down stitch line, with thread under needle point. Continue in this way.

Detached chain stitch or daisy stitch

This is worked in a similar way as chain stitch, but each loop is tied with a vertical stitch.

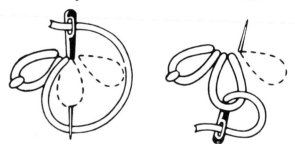

Open chain stitch

Bring thread through at A and hold down with left thumb. Insert needle at B and bring out again at C, with needle point above thread. Leave loop fairly loose and insert needle inside loop at D.

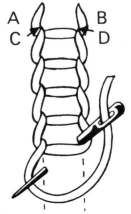

Chevron stitch

Bring the needle through on the lower line at the left side of work, and insert a little to the right on the same line. Take a small stitch to the left emerging at the midway point of the stitch being made. Insert the needle on the upper line a little to the right, and take a small stitch to the left, as shown in diagram 1. Insert the needle again on the same line a little to the right and take a small stitch to the left, emerging at centre as in diagram 2. Continue to work in this way alternately on the upper and lower lines.

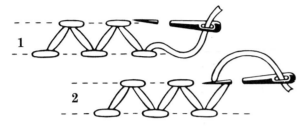

Couching

Bring thread to be couched through from back to front of fabric and lay it along stitch line. With couching thread (usually a thinner one) make tiny stitches over other thread at regular intervals to hold it firmly in place.

An example of simple couching in metal threads and wool on a cream background.

Cretan stitch

Bring needle through just above the centre of the space to be filled at left side. With thread to right, insert needle at lower edge and bring out just below centre with needle point above

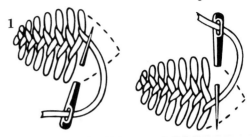

thread (diagram 1). With thread to right again, insert needle at top edge and bring out just above centre, with needle point over thread. This stitch can also be worked open (diagram 2).

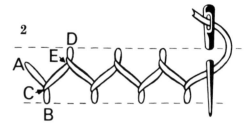

Double knot stitch

Bring the needle through at A on diagram 1. Take a small stitch across the line at B. Pass the needle downwards under the surface stitch just made, without piercing the fabric, as at C. With the thread under the needle, pass the needle again under the first stitch at D. Pull the thread through to form a knot. The knots should be spaced evenly and closely to obtain a beaded effect.

Feather stitch

Bring needle out at top of stitch line. Holding thread down with left thumb, insert needle a

little to the right and bring out above thread a short distance down in the centre. Insert to the left and bring out above thread a little lower down (diagram 1). Double feather stitch has two stitches to the right and two to the left (diagram 2).

Fern stitch

This consists of three straight stitches (see page 14) of equal length radiating from the same central point. Bring needle through at A and make a straight stitch to B. Bring the needle through again at A and make another straight stitch to C. Repeat once more at D and bring the needle through at E to begin the next three radiating stitches. The central stitch follows the line of the design. This stitch may also be used in counted-thread embroidery on evenweave fabric.

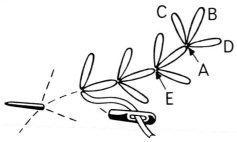

Fly stitch

Begin at top of stitch line and bring needle through a little to the left. Holding thread down with left thumb, insert needle an equal distance to the right of stitch line and bring out again on stitch line a short distance down. Make a short vertical stitch downwards, then bring needle out ready for next stitch. This stitch can be worked in rows or individually. When a single stitch is being made the vertical stitch is very tiny.

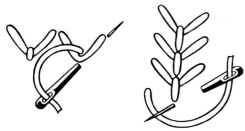

French knot

Bring needle through fabric and hold thread down with left thumb. Twist thread twice round needle. Still holding thread firmly turn needle and insert close to starting point. Pull tightly.

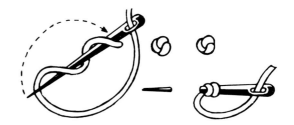

Herringbone stitch

Work from left to right. Bring needle out at bottom of area where stitching is to appear. Insert at top and to the right, take a small stitch to the left then insert back at bottom. Ideally the stitch taken up by the needle should be the same length as the space between stitches.

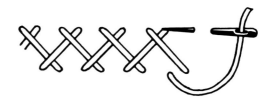

Long and short stitch

This form of satin stitch is so named as all the stitches are of varying lengths. It is often used to fill a shape which is too large or too irregular to be covered by satin stitch. It is also used to achieve a shaded effect. In the first row the stitches are alternately long and short and closely follow the outline of the shape. The stitches in

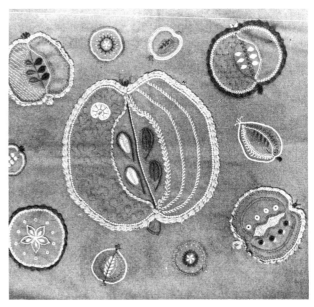

Each motif in this sample is based on an apple shape, treated with different surface stitchery.

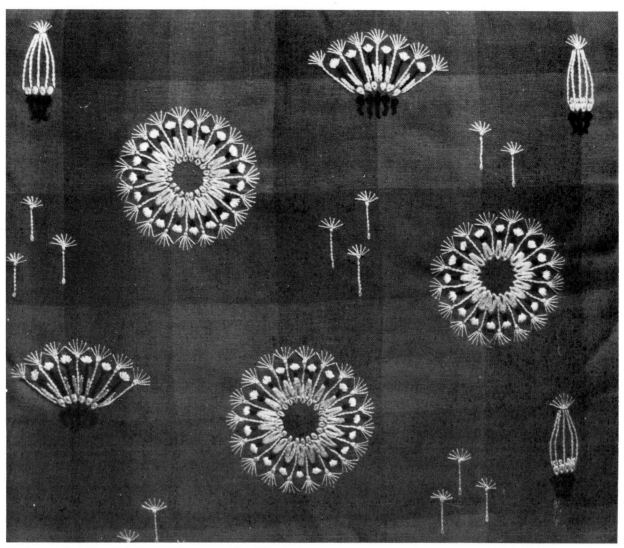

A checked cotton fabric was used as the background for this embroidery. The circular and curved motifs, worked in a variety of surface stitches, make a pleasing contrast against the squares of the fabric.

the following rows are worked to achieve a smooth appearance.

Overcast stitch

Work from left to right. Bring needle through just below stitch line and insert it just above. Bring it out again just below stitch line a little

to the right. Continue in this way, following stitch line and working stitches close together.

Pekinese stitch
illustrated overleaf

Work back stitch in the usual way (see page 9), then interlace with toning or contrasting thread. The stitch is shown open in the diagram but the loops should be pulled slightly when working.

Running stitch

Work from right to left. Bring needle through on stitch line and take it over three or four threads of the fabric then under one or two threads. Continue in this way, keeping all the same length, and all the spaces the same. This stitch can be threaded in the same way as for back stitch.

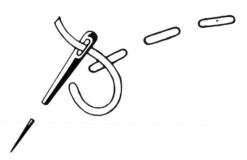

Satin stitch

Work straight stitches (see below) close together across space to be filled, bringing needle out for each new stitch only a thread of the fabric beyond previous stitch so you get a solid shape of stitching.

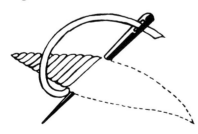

Satin stitch, padded

This is often used for working monograms and initials, when a slightly raised, well-padded surface is required. Outline the design first of all with small running stitches, then work chain stitches to cover the area completely – begin the chain stitches just inside line of running stitches and work in towards the centre. Finally cover the area with satin stitches, worked close together and all slanting in the same direction.

Split stitch

Bring the needle through at left-hand side of work. Make a small stitch over the line of the design, piercing the working thread with the needle, as shown in the diagram below.

Stem stitch

Work from left to right. Bring needle out on stitch line then insert a little way along and slightly below line. Bring needle up a little way back just above stitch line. Continue in this way.

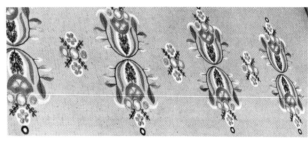

Motifs for an embroidered bedspread, worked mainly in stem, chain and satin stitch, and French knots.

Straight stitch

Bring needle through at bottom of stitch area, insert at top then bring out at bottom of next stitch. Continue in this way. Straight stitches can be worked to form any shape or fill any area.

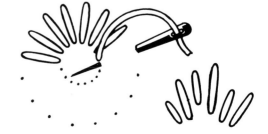

SHADOW WORK

This is a delicate and pleasing form of embroidery, particularly effective for children's party dresses, and fragile dressing-table mats, although it can be used for many other purposes too. As the name suggests the embroidery appears in 'shadow' – this is achieved by using transparent fabric and working the stitching on the wrong side of the fabric. Closed herringbone stitch is always used for this work, but if wished the work can be highlighted with further stitching detail by working directly on to the right side of the fabric.

Traditionally shadow work designs were always worked on organdie, but now there are many attractive synthetic and natural fabrics available which give beautiful delicate effects. Take care however, if you are following a shadow work pattern, to ensure the fabric you buy is of the correct width – usually cotton organdie, for instance, is only supplied in 45-in. widths, nylon organdie is 36 in. wide. Shadow work on muslin is particularly effective.

Shadow work was once always worked in white thread on white fabric, but the introduction of coloured threads into the embroidery can considerably vary its appearance. Bright colours used on the back of a pale transparent fabric create an almost opalescent effect on the front.

Shadow work monogram worked on fine muslin.

Stem, back, satin, straight stitches, and French knots, are the stitches most often combined with shadow work, and are usually worked on the right side of the fabric.

To work shadow work stitch

This can either be worked on the right side of fabric as a double back stitch, or on the wrong side of fabric as closed herringbone stitch. Diagram 1 shows the double back stitch version: a small back stitch is worked alternately on each side of the traced double lines (the dotted lines on the diagram show the formation of the thread on the wrong side of the fabric). The colour of the thread appears delicately through the fabric. Diagram 2 shows the stitch worked on the wrong side of the fabric as a closed herringbone stitch with no spaces left between the stitches. Both methods achieve the same result.

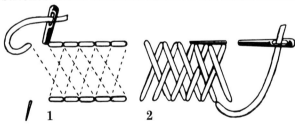

CUTWORK

This is a specialised type of free embroidery in which flowers, leaves and figures are surrounded by buttonhole stitch, sometimes joined by bars and then certain areas of the fabric are cut away to give a lace-like effect. Sometimes surface stitchery is added to enhance the embroidery.

Cutwork, in a variety of styles and patterns, has been popular since the sixteenth century when it reached a particular peak of popularity; many fine examples can be seen in the portraits of the time. The fashion spread from Italy and many of the methods and stitches still bear Italian names, such as Renaissance, Venetian and Reticella. The French developed their own style in cutwork which is widely known as Richelieu cutwork.

A fairly firm linen or similar fabric should be used for cutwork – if the fabric is too flimsy it will be difficult to cut away areas cleanly. And a small pair of well-sharpened, pointed scissors will be required.

Begin by transferring your design in any of the usual ways. Work a double line of running stitches round outline of design to emphasise and strengthen it. Now work buttonhole stitch closely over the edge of the outline of the design, having the 'head' of the buttonhole stitch at the edge which will be cut. Finally when all the design has been stitched, trim away the unwanted areas of fabric. Work on the right side of fabric, and take care not to snip the stitches as you cut.

Buttonhole stitch bars

These bars occur frequently in conventional cutwork and in Richelieu work. Make a row of running stitches between the double lines of the design as a padding for the buttonhole stitch. Where a single line bar is required, take a thread across the space and back. securing with a small stitch and buttonhole stitch closely over the loose threads without picking up any of the fabric (diagram 1). Buttonhole stitch round the shape, keeping the looped edges of the stitch to the inside, then cut away the fabric from behind the bar and round the inside of the shape. Where a double line or a broad bar is required between shapes, or sometimes for stems of flowers when the fabric is to be cut away on each side, make a row of running stitches along the centre, then buttonhole stitch along one side spacing the stitches slightly. Buttonhole stitch along the other side into the spaces left by the first row. The fabric is then cut away close to the buttonhole stitch leaving a strong broad bar (diagram 2).

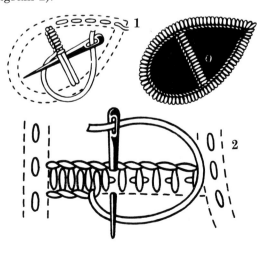

A fine white linen tablecloth with a circular pattern of cutwork embroidery.

THE PATTERNS

Giraffe motif for a child's dress

MATERIALS
Of Clark's Anchor Stranded Cotton (USA J. & P. Coats Deluxe Six Strand Floss) — 1 skein each Terra Cotta 0339/430, Nasturtium 0330/545, Jade 0188/524, White 0402 and Black 0403. A child's box-pleated dress, in a suitable plain pale green fabric (or colour required). A Milward 'Gold Seal' crewel needle No. 6.

STITCHES
Satin; straight; French knots; twisted chain (see below).

DIAGRAMS
Diagram A gives the giraffe and flower in actual size.
Diagram B gives a guide to the stitches and thread colours used throughout the design.
Diagram C shows how to work twisted chain stitch: begin as for ordinary chain stitch, but instead of inserting the needle into the place from where it emerged, insert it close to the last loop and take a small slanting stitch coming out on the line of the design. Pull the thread through. The loops of this stitch should be worked closely together to have the correct effect.

TO MAKE
Note. Use 3 strands of cotton throughout.
Trace the giraffe motif from diagram A, omitting flowers, centrally on left-hand pleat of dress 2 in. from lower edge. Trace in reverse on to right-hand pleat. Scatter large and small flower motifs on dress, in any positions wished. Work embroidery, following diagram B and stitch and colour key. Unnumbered parts on diagram B are worked in the same stitch and colour as the numbered parts most similar to them.

TO COMPLETE
Press embroidery on the wrong side.

STITCH AND COLOUR KEY
1	Nasturtium	Satin stitch
2	Jade	Satin stitch
3	White	Straight stitch
4	Terra Cotta	Straight stitch
5	Black	Straight stitch
6	Black	French knots
7	Terra cotta	Twisted chain stitch

Diagram B

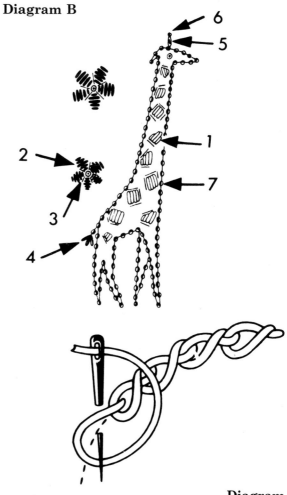

Diagram A

Diagram C

19

Above: *a 19th-century Chinese embroidered panel, worked mainly in satin stitch.*

Opposite: *a pretty shadow work pattern worked on a ground of pale blue organdie.*

round lower edge, and draw up gathers to fit over main section of holder. Stitch to outside of main section $\frac{3}{4}$ in. from top edge. Make up other frill in a similar way and attach to lower edge of main section. Make up bands from remaining pieces of fabric, each to be $\frac{1}{2}$ in. wide —i.e. fold strip in half lengthwise, right sides together, and stitch long edges together with $\frac{1}{2}$-in. turnings. Turn right side out and press well. Stitch one band over base of each frill.

STITCH KEY
1 Satin stitch
2 French knots
3 Stem stitch
4 Back stitch
5 Straight stitch
6 Fly stitch
7 Feather stitch
8 Chain stitch

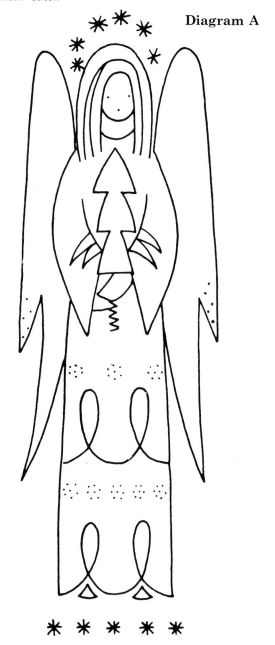

Diagram A

Christmas napkin holder

MATERIALS
One 10-gram ball Clark's Anchor Pearl Cotton No. 8 in White 0402 *or* 1 skein Clark's Anchor Stranded Cotton (USA J. & P. Coats Deluxe Six Strand Floss) in White 0402. $\frac{1}{4}$ yd. red cotton or poplin, 36 in. wide. A cylinder of stiff cardboard, 9 in. long and $1\frac{1}{2}$ in. in diameter. A Milward 'Gold Seal' crewel needle No. 6.

STITCHES
Satin; French knots; stem; back; straight; fly; feather; chain.

DIAGRAMS
Diagram A gives the complete design in actual size.
Diagram B gives a guide to the stitches used throughout the design.

TO MAKE
Note. If using stranded cotton, use 3 strands throughout.
Cut one large piece from fabric, 10 in. by 6 in. Cut two pieces, each 3 in. by $11\frac{1}{2}$ in., and two pieces, each $1\frac{1}{2}$ in. by 6 in. Trace design as given in diagram A centrally on to large piece of fabric. Work embroidery, following diagram B and stitch and colour key. Unnumbered parts on diagram B are worked in the same stitch and colour as the numbered parts most similar to them.

TO COMPLETE
Press embroidery on the wrong side. Machine stitch long sides of main section together, right sides facing, to fit cardboard cylinder. Turn in $\frac{1}{2}$ in. at each end and stitch in position. Turn right side out. Insert cardboard cylinder. Join short sides of one frill section, right sides together. Turn right side out and turn in and stitch a small hem along top edge. Work two rows of gathering stitches

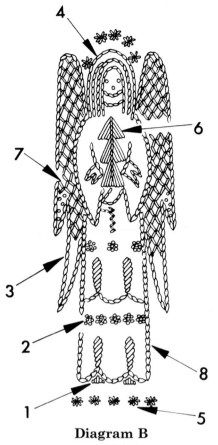

Diagram B

Tissue holder

MATERIALS
Of Clark's Anchor Pearl Cotton No. 8 — one 10-gram ball each Gorse Yellow 0301/442 and Black 0403 *or* of Clark's Anchor Stranded Cotton (USA J. & P. Coats Deluxe Six Strand Floss) — 1 skein each Gorse Yellow 0301/442 and Black 0403. Piece of green poplin, or other suitable fabric, 6 in. by $7\frac{1}{4}$ in. A 6-in. square of non-woven iron-on interfacing. A Milward 'Gold Seal' crewel needle No. 6.

STITCHES
Satin; French knots; double knot; back.

DIAGRAMS *(see page 25)*
Diagram A gives one complete motif in actual size.
Diagram B gives a guide to the stitches and colours used throughout the design.

TO MAKE
Note. If using stranded cotton, then use 3 strands throughout.

With one long side of fabric facing, trace the motif as given in diagram A centrally on to fabric, $\frac{5}{8}$ in. from one side edge. Repeat at other end of fabric. Work embroidery, following diagram B and stitch and colour key. Unnumbered parts on diagram B are worked in the same stitch and colour as the numbered parts most similar to them.

TO COMPLETE
Press embroidery on the wrong side. Turn in $\frac{1}{2}$ in. on side edges and press. Iron interfacing centrally on to wrong side, overlapping turned-in edges. Fold sides to the centre, right sides together, and machine stitch $\frac{1}{4}$ in. from raw edges. Turn right side out.

A traditional counted-thread design worked in satin and back stitch.

Diagram A

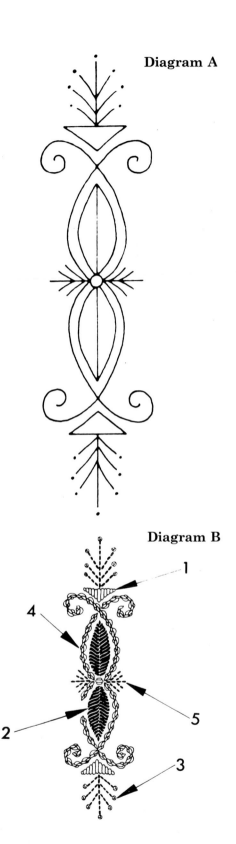

Diagram B

STITCH AND COLOUR KEY

1	Gorse Yellow	Satin stitch
2	Black	Satin stitch
3	Gorse Yellow	French knots
4	Gorse Yellow	Double knot stitch
5	Black	Back stitch

Shadow work used to decorate bathroom curtains.

Long cushion

MATERIALS

Of Clark's Anchor Stranded Cotton (USA J. &. P. Coats Deluxe Six Strand Floss) — 2 skeins each Dark Parma Violet 0112/450 and Black 0403, 1 skein each Pale Parma Violet 0108/447, Mid Parma Violet 0110/448, Jade 0188/524, Muscat Green 0281/786, and Grey 0400. ¾ yd. white mediumweight slub linen, 36 in. wide. A Milward 'Gold Seal' crewel needle No. 6. A cushion pad, 22 in. by 14 in.

STITCHES

Stem; satin; back; long and short; buttonhole; straight; French knots; double knot.

DIAGRAMS

Diagram A gives one half of the complete design in actual size.
Diagram B (page 28) gives a guide to the stitches and colours used throughout the design.

TO MAKE

Note. Use 3 strands of cotton throughout.
Cut two pieces from fabric, each 23 in. by 15 in. Fold one piece across the centre widthwise and crease lightly to mark. Trace the design as given in diagram A centrally on to fold of fabric. The broken line on the diagram should coincide with your fabric fold line. Turn fabric and repeat design on other side of fold.
Work embroidery following diagram B and stitch and colour key. Unnumbered parts on diagram B are worked in the same stitch and colour as the numbered parts most similar to them.

TO COMPLETE

Press the embroidery on the wrong side. Place both fabric sections together, right sides facing, and machine stitch round all edges, with ½-in. turnings. Leave a gap in one seam; turn cover to right side through this gap, and insert cushion pad. Turn in seam allowance on the remaining open edges and slipstitch neatly together.

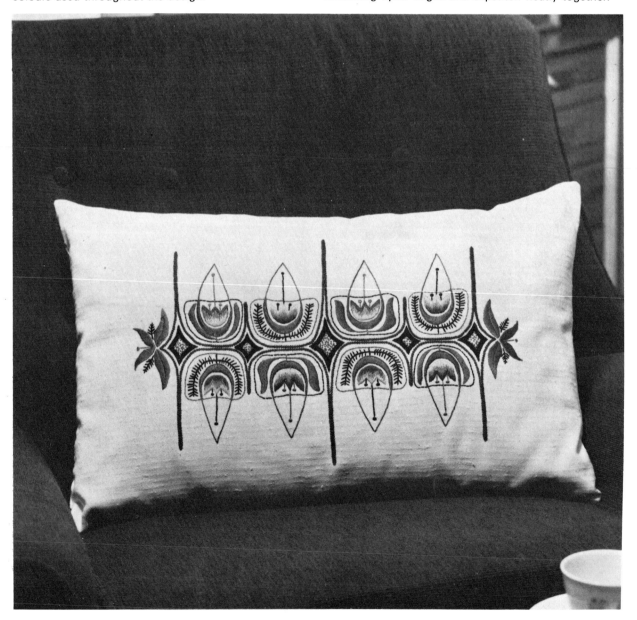

Diagram A

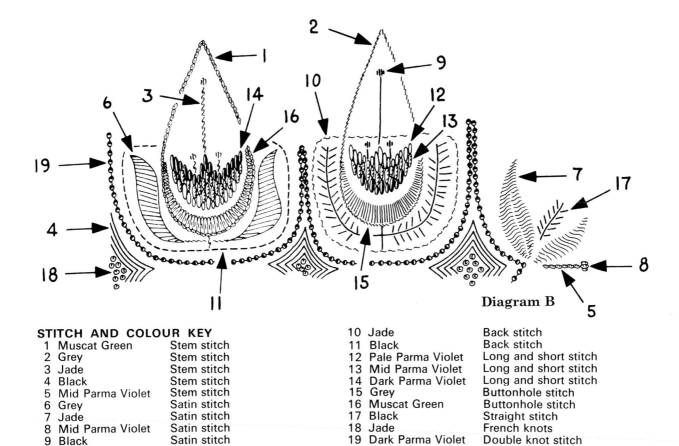

Diagram B

STITCH AND COLOUR KEY

1 Muscat Green	Stem stitch	
2 Grey	Stem stitch	
3 Jade	Stem stitch	
4 Black	Stem stitch	
5 Mid Parma Violet	Stem stitch	
6 Grey	Satin stitch	
7 Jade	Satin stitch	
8 Mid Parma Violet	Satin stitch	
9 Black	Satin stitch	
10 Jade	Back stitch	
11 Black	Back stitch	
12 Pale Parma Violet	Long and short stitch	
13 Mid Parma Violet	Long and short stitch	
14 Dark Parma Violet	Long and short stitch	
15 Grey	Buttonhole stitch	
16 Muscat Green	Buttonhole stitch	
17 Black	Straight stitch	
18 Jade	French knots	
19 Dark Parma Violet	Double knot stitch	

A church kneeler embroidered in needlepoint tapestry stitches.

Tablecloth embroidered with a traditional Hardanger design.

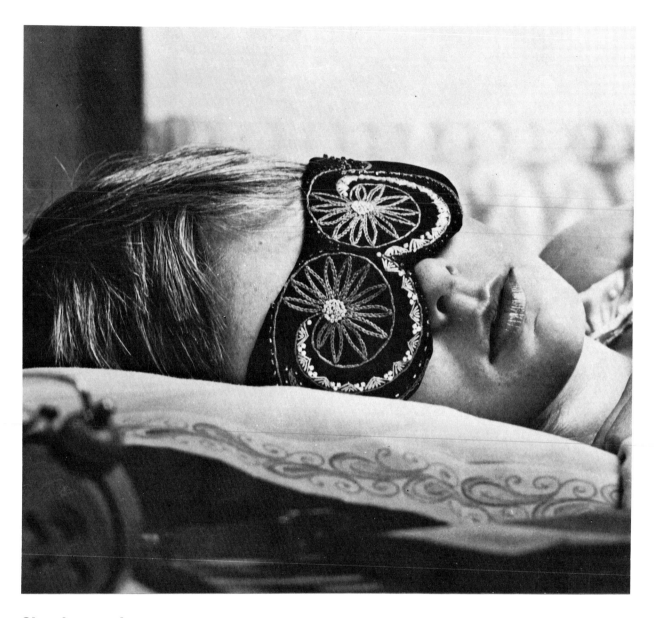

Sleeping mask

MATERIALS
Of Clark's Anchor Stranded Cotton (J. & P. Coats
Deluxe Six Strand Floss) — 1 skein each Cyclamen 089,
Cobalt Blue 0129, and Jade 0187. 53 small pearls, and
106 small green glass beads. Piece of close-weave
black grosgrain or other suitable fabric, 10 in. by 5 in.
Piece of fine black fabric for lining, 10 in. by 5 in. 1¼ yd.
black ribbon, ½ in. wide, for ties. A Milward 'Gold Seal'
crewel needle No. 24.

STITCHES
Chain; couching; fly; straight; French knots.

DIAGRAMS
Diagram A gives one, half of the complete design in
actual size.
Diagram B gives a guide to the stitches and colours
used throughout the design.

TO MAKE
Note. In couching, use 4 strands of cotton for laid thread,
2 strands for tying stitch; use 3 strands of cotton for rest
of embroidery.
Fold fabric across the centre widthwise and crease lightly.
With one long side of fabric facing, trace the design as
given in diagram A on to right-hand side of fabric. The
broken line on the diagram should coincide with your
centre fold. Trace the design in reverse on to left-hand
side of fabric. Work embroidery, following diagram B
and stitch and colour key. Unnumbered parts on
diagram B are worked in the same stitch and colour as the
numbered parts most similar to them.

TO COMPLETE
Press the embroidery on the wrong side. Sew on beads,
using a matching thread, and following diagram B
'for position of pearls and beads. Trim embroidered piece
to within ½ in. from broken outline. Trim lining fabric
to match. Cut ribbon in half. Place embroidered piece
and lining fabric together, wrong sides facing. Turn
in seam allowances and slipstitch neatly together.
Insert ribbons at upper corners as you stitch.

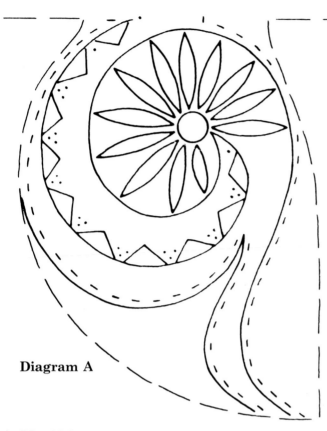

Diagram A

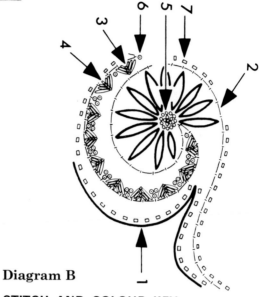

Diagram B

STITCH AND COLOUR KEY
1	Cyclamen	Chain stitch
2	Jade	Couching
3	Cobalt Blue	Fly stitch
4	Cobalt Blue	Straight stitch
5	Cobalt Blue	French knots
6		Pearls
7		Beads

Motif for stockings

MATERIALS
One 10-gram ball Clark's Anchor Pearl Cotton No. 8 in Black 0403 *or* 3 skeins Clark's Anchor Stranded Cotton (USA J. & P. Coats Deluxe Six Strand Floss) in Black 0403. A pair of white stockings or tights. A Milward 'Gold Seal' crewel needle No. 6.

STITCHES
Double knot; satin.

DIAGRAMS
Diagram A gives one complete motif in actual size.
Diagram B gives a guide to the stitches used throughout the design.

TO MAKE
Note. If using stranded cotton, then use 3 strands throughout.
Trace the motif as given in diagram A four times on to centre front fold of each stocking, with the first motif 4 in. from the top and spacing other motifs at $5\frac{1}{4}$-in. intervals. Repeat motifs on each side of centre fold, spacing alternately as shown in photograph. Work embroidery, following diagram B and stitch key. Unnumbered parts on diagram B are worked in the same stitch as the numbered parts most similar to them.

STITCH KEY
1 Double knot stitch
2 Satin stitch

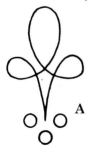

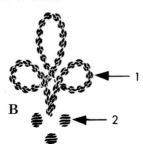

31

Sampler worked in cross and Holbein stitches.

Umbrella cover

MATERIALS

Of Clark's Anchor Stranded Cotton (USA J. & P. Coats Deluxe Six Strand Floss) — 1 skein each Almond Green 0259, Moss Green 0269/955, Terra Cotta 0339/430, and Black 0403. $\frac{1}{4}$ yd. grey nylon or rayon fabric, 36 in. wide. One 5-in. nylon zip fastener to match fabric. A Milward 'Gold Seal' crewel needle No. 6.

STITCHES

Stem; satin; French knots; back; buttonhole.

DIAGRAMS

Diagram A gives one large motif and one small motif in actual size.
Diagram B gives a guide to the stitches and colours used throughout the design.

TO MAKE

Note. Use 3 strands of cotton throughout.
Cut $5\frac{1}{4}$ in. from short end of fabric for cuff of cover. Trace large motif as given in diagram A centrally on to remaining fabric, $2\frac{1}{4}$ in. from top edge. Repeat in reverse $\frac{1}{2}$ in. under first motif. Trace small motif 1 in. from previous motif, and then again in reverse $1\frac{1}{2}$ in. from first small motif. Work embroidery, following diagram B and stitch and colour key. Unnumbered parts on diagram B are worked in the same stitch and colour as the numbered parts most similar to them.

TO COMPLETE

Press the embroidery on the wrong side. Place the embroidered section round the umbrella, wrong side out, and pin to fit. Trim, leaving $\frac{1}{2}$-in. seam allowances on all edges. Turn up $\frac{1}{4}$-in. hem at lower edge. Stitch long seam, right sides together, leaving 5 in. unstitched at the top for the zip. Turn to right side and insert zip into opening. Fold cuff section in half lengthwise and trim to fit top edge of cover, allowing $\frac{1}{4}$-in. seam allowance for side seams. With right sides facing, machine stitch side seams of cuff. Turn to right side. Place single edge of cuff to edge of cover, right sides together and stitch. Turn in remaining raw edge and slipstitch in place to seam just stitched.

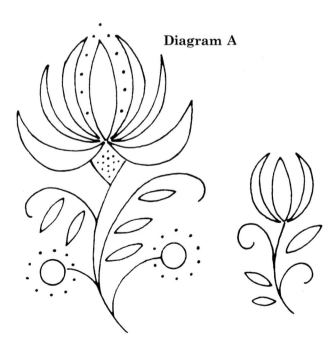

Diagram A

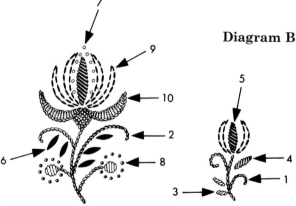

Diagram B

STITCH AND COLOUR KEY

1	Moss Green	Stem stitch
2	Terra Cotta	Stem stitch
3	Almond Green	Satin stitch
4	Moss Green	Satin stitch
5	Terra Cotta	Satin stitch
6	Black	Satin stitch
7	Almond Green	French knots
8	Terra Cotta	French knots
9	Black	Back stitch
10	Terra Cotta	Buttonhole stitch

Beaded trimming for a jacket

MATERIALS
Of Clark's Anchor Stranded Cotton (USA J. &. P. Coats Deluxe Six Strand Floss) – 1 skein each Carnation 023/526, Violet 095/411, Cobalt Blue 0129/592, Grass Green 0243/498, and Buttercup 0293/582. Small glass beads, approximately $\frac{1}{16}$ in. long. Small pearls, approximately $\frac{1}{8}$ in. in diameter. A suitable white or light-coloured edge-to-edge jacket, with high round neck and long sleeves. A beading needle.

DIAGRAMS
Diagram A gives a section of the design in actual size.
Diagram B shows the arrangement of the beaded stitches and pearls on the fabric.
Diagram C shows how to work beading stitches: bring the needle through and slip the beads one by one along the needle; insert the needle into the fabric the required distance away along line of design.

TO MAKE
Note. Use 2 strands of cotton throughout.
Trace the section of the design as given in diagram A on to lower right-hand front of jacket, $\frac{1}{2}$ in. from edges. Omitting section of design within dotted line, repeat the design in reverse directly above the section already traced, in position indicated by broken line. Trace in reverse on to left-hand front, then continue design round neck edge adjusting as necessary to fit curve of neckline. Trace design round lower edge of each sleeve. Work beading stitches as indicated in diagram B. Use green cotton for all the stems and leaves; alternate the other colours on the flower heads.

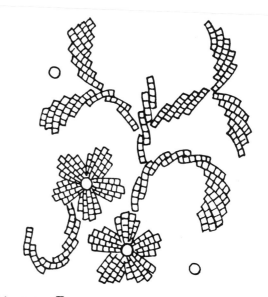

Diagram B

Diagram A

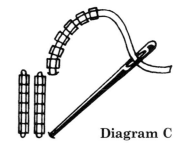

Diagram C

34

His and hers guest towels

MATERIALS
Of Clark's Anchor Stranded Cotton (USA J. & P. Coats Deluxe Six Strand Floss) – 1 skein White 0402. Two huckaback guest towels, each 15 in. by 22 in., in deep pink (or colour preferred). A Milward 'Gold Seal' crewel needle No. 6.

STITCH
Satin.

DIAGRAMS
Diagram A gives the 'his' and 'hers' motifs in actual size.
Diagram B shows the arrangement of satin stitches on each letter.

TO MAKE
Note. Use 3 strands of cotton throughout
Trace each word centrally on to each towel, 1½ in. up from lower edge. The embroidery is worked throughout in satin stitches – follow diagram B for the arrangement of stitches on each letter.

TO COMPLETE
Press embroidery on the wrong side.

Diagram A

Diagram B

Diagram A

Shadow work cheval set

MATERIALS
Of Clark's Anchor Stranded Cotton (USA J. &. P. Coats Deluxe Six Strand Floss) — 2 skeins Cyclamen 088, 1 skein Moss Green 0267. ½ yd. white organdie or other similar transparent fabric, 36 in. wide. A Milward 'Gold Seal' crewel needle No. 7.

STITCHES
Shadow work stitch (see page 16); stem; satin; French knots; blanket; back.

DIAGRAMS
Diagram A gives the complete motif in actual size.
Diagram B (see page 38) gives a guide to the stitches and thread colours used throughout the design.

TO MAKE
Note. Use 3 strands of cotton throughout.
Cut one piece from fabric, 11 in. by 21 in., and two pieces each 8½ in. square. With one long side of large piece facing, trace motif as given in diagram A on to bottom left-hand corner, 1½ in. from side edge and 1¾ in. from lower edge. Trace motif at right-hand corner to correspond. Trace the flower head centrally on to each square of fabric, omitting stem and leaves and tracing one more small motif between petals to complete the design.
Work embroidery, following diagram B and stitch and colour key. Unnumbered parts on diagram B are worked in the same stitch and colour as the numbered parts most similar to them.

TO COMPLETE

Press embroidery on the wrong side. Turn in $\frac{1}{4}$-in. hems on all edges of each mat, and slipstitch neatly in place.

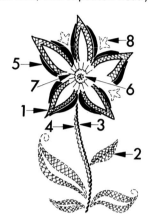

Diagram B

STITCH AND COLOUR KEY
1 Cyclamen   Shadow work stitch
2 Moss Green   Shadow work stitch
3 Cyclamen   Stem stitch
4 Moss Green   Stem stitch
5 Cyclamen   Satin stitch
6 Cyclamen   French knots
7 Moss Green   Blanket stitch
8 Moss Green   Back stitch

Cutwork trolley cloth

MATERIALS
Of Clark's Anchor Pearl Cotton No. 8 — one 10-gram ball each Pale Geranium 08/734, Mid Geranium 011/382, Mid Moss Green 0266/789, Dark Moss Green 0268/954, and Gorse Yellow 0301/442. $\frac{5}{8}$ yd. fine white embroidery linen, 36 in. wide. A Milward 'Gold Seal' crewel needle No. 6.

STITCHES
Buttonhole; stem; satin.

DIAGRAMS
Diagram A gives one complete motif of the design in actual size.
Diagram B gives a guide to the stitches and thread colours used throughout the design.

TO MAKE
Cut one piece from fabric, 28 in. by 20 in. Fold fabric across the centre both ways and crease lightly. With one short side of fabric facing, trace motif as given in diagram A on to right-hand side of fabric, 9 in. below widthwise fold. The large broken line on the diagram indicates the lengthwise fold, and should coincide with your fold line. To complete short side, turn fabric and omitting double side lines, trace left-hand side to correspond. The small broken line on the diagram indicates the position and outline of the start of the second motif. Trace other short side of fabric in a similar way, then join up double lines at the side edges. Work embroidery, following diagram B and stitch and colour key. Unnumbered parts on diagram B are worked in the same stitch and colour as the numbered parts most similar to them.

TO COMPLETE
Press embroidery on the wrong side. Cut away all sections marked 'X' on diagram A, and trim away surplus fabric round the outside edge, using small, sharp-pointed scissors. Cut from the wrong side, taking care not to snip stitches.

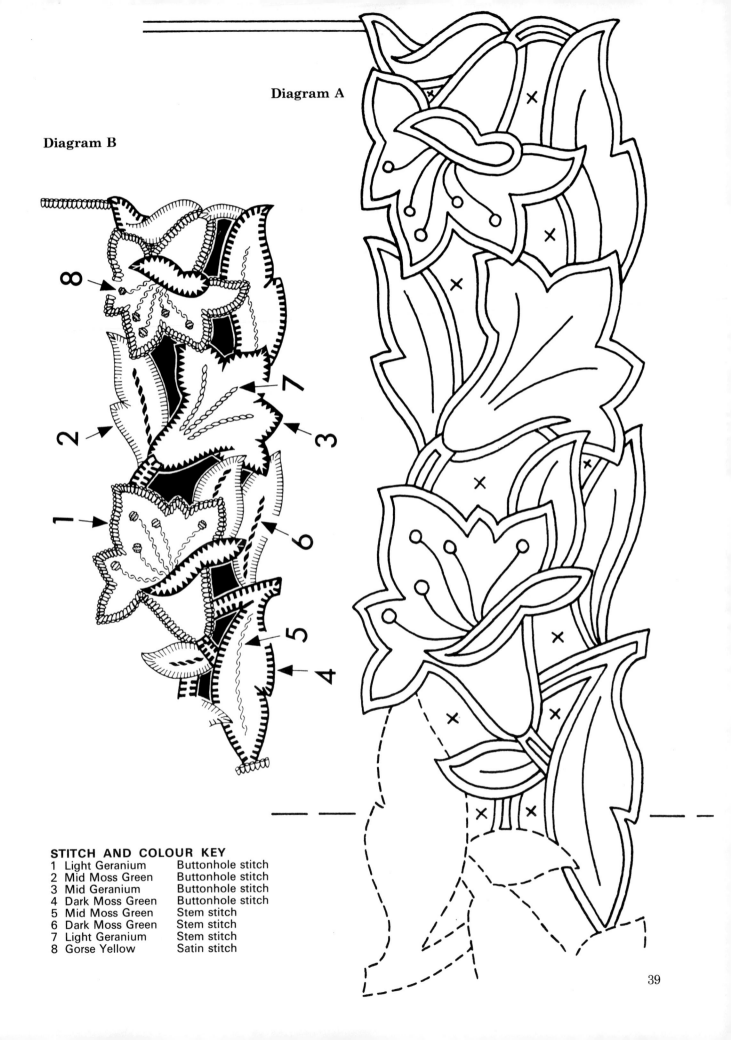

Diagram A

Diagram B

8

2

1

7

3

6

5

4

STITCH AND COLOUR KEY
1 Light Geranium   Buttonhole stitch
2 Mid Moss Green   Buttonhole stitch
3 Mid Geranium   Buttonhole stitch
4 Dark Moss Green   Buttonhole stitch
5 Mid Moss Green   Stem stitch
6 Dark Moss Green   Stem stitch
7 Light Geranium   Stem stitch
8 Gorse Yellow   Satin stitch

Chapter two
COUNTED-THREAD EMBROIDERY

An Italian, 16th-century embroidered panel, worked in drawn-thread stitches.

The principal difference between free-style embroidery and counted-thread work is that in free-style work the design must be drawn on to the fabric by tracing or some other suitable method; in counted-thread embroidery this is not necessary. A design is formed by worked stitches over specific numbers of the threads of the fabric. For this reason it is necessary to use an evenweave fabric in which warp and weft threads are clearly defined and easy to count. Most counted-thread designs are presented in chart form, with each line on the chart representing one thread of your fabric. Stitches are then indicated on the chart to cover different numbers of threads.

In free-style embroidery almost any type of design is acceptable, abstract or representative; in counted-thread work, as the mesh of the fabric imposes limitations, designs tend to be more geometric in form and are therefore usually more symmetrical and uniform than free-style patterns.

Many traditional styles of embroidery, including cross stitch, drawn-fabric and drawn-thread work, as well as innumerable national embroideries, are based on count-thread work. A few of these are described later in this chapter.

Before embarking on any counted-thread design, it is essential to prepare your fabric very carefully. As the entire design is based on the accurate counting out of fabric threads, if you miscount by even one or two threads, the result will be an out-of-true and unbalanced design.

Beginners should start with a very coarse mesh fabric, in which fabric threads are easy to see and to count. From this you can progress to finer meshes and more intricate designs. Evenweave linen, net, huckaback and hessian (burlap) are all suitable fabrics to use.

Begin by cutting your fabric to the size required, remembering to allow extra for hems or seams. Machine stitch or oversew along cut edges to prevent them fraying. Now work lines of basting stitches lengthwise and widthwise across the exact centre of the fabric. These lines will act as a guide when placing the design. As a further guide it is a good idea to mark out threads in groups of ten or eight along the top and down one side of the fabric. Take basting stitches alternately over then under each group.

STITCHES TO USE

Many traditional forms of counted-thread embroidery will use only one or sometimes two stitches throughout the whole design. Others are created from a variety of different stitches. The following is a selection of general-purpose counted-thread stitches – others which relate to specific techniques are described under the appropriate heading. There are also a number of free-style stitches which can be adapted for use in counted-thread work – for instance, cable, fern, chevron, fly, double knot and Pekinese (see chapter one for these stitches). And most of the stitches used in needlepoint tapestry (see chapter three) can also be used for counted-thread work on evenweave fabric. In most cases however where a canvas stitch is worked over only one or two threads of canvas, it will be worked over several threads of fabric.

Back stitch

Stitches should be worked over a regular number of threads throughout a design. Bring needle out on the right-hand side of work two threads (or the required number) to the left of the fabric edge. Take a backward stitch over this number of threads and bring the needle through two threads in front of the previous stitch. Continue in this way, always returning the needle in a backward stitch into the same place where it last emerged.

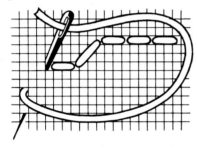

Back stitch, whipped

Work back stitch first, as described above, then with another thread in the needle whip over each back stitch without entering the fabric.

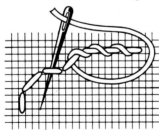

Darning

The simple darning stitch forms the basis for a number of decorative embroidery styles. Usually a design will be worked entirely in darning

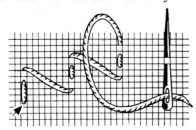

stitches, although the length of the individual stitches may vary according to the requirements of the design. Work from right to left, or left to right, in rows, weaving thread over and under the required number of threads. The diagram shows one arrangement of darning stitches frequently found in Swedish darning designs.

Diagonal raised band

This stitch is worked diagonally from lower right to top left corner. Bring needle out at the arrow on diagram 1. Insert four threads up (A) and bring out two threads down and two threads to the left (B). Continue in this way to the end of the row. Diagram 2 shows the second stage in working the band. After completing the last stitch at the end of the first (upward) row, bring the needle through as if to commence a further stitch. Take the needle horizontally across the last stitch worked and insert four threads to the right (C). Bring needle through two threads down, and two to the left (D). Continue to the end of the row. Pull all stitches firmly.

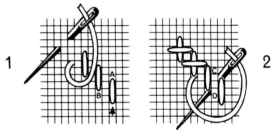

Holbein or double running stitch

Work a row of running stitches (see page 14) with the spaces between stitches the same length as the stitches themselves. Work a return journey of running stitches, filling in the gaps left on the first row. This gives a continuous line of even stitches.

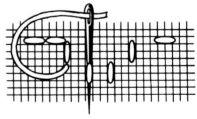

Mosaic filling

Work four blocks of satin stitches to form a square, with an equal number of stitches in each block and worked over an equal number of

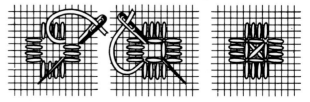

threads. Bring the needle from the last stitch through to the right-hand corner of the inner square. Work a four-sided stitch (see page 45) within the satin stitch blocks, bringing the needle out at the starting point. Now work a basic cross stitch (see right) in the centre.

Satin stitch

Another free-style stitch which can be used in counted-thread designs. Work from right to left, or left to right. The number of threads over which the stitches are worked may vary depending upon the effect desired. When satin stitch is worked in counted-thread designs, it is often termed counted satin stitch. It forms the basis for several different national styles of embroidery.

Straight stitch

Single stitches are worked over two threads. The stitches may be horizontal, vertical or diagonal.

Pin cushion in counted satin stitch.

CROSS STITCH WORK

Cross stitch can be used in free, counted-thread and canvas embroidery, but as it is the basis for so many traditional embroidery styles, and the stitch itself has so many variations, cross stitch work has in a way become a technique in itself.

Some beautiful examples of cross stitch work have been found in peasant embroideries throughout the world; some are worked in wonderfully vivid colours, others are delicate and muted. Often a design is worked entirely in cross stitch only, but the stitch can be effectively combined with one or two other counted-thread stitches – for instance, in Assisi and Roumanian work (see pages 46 and 47) where it is combined with Holbein stitch.

To work the basic cross stitch

When working cross stitch on canvas, in order not to distort the canvas threads, each complete cross must be completed before moving to the next. But on evenweave fabric, where there is no danger of distortion, it is possible to work cross stitch in rows; bring needle out at bottom right edge of row. Insert four threads up and four threads to the left (or number of threads over which you are working the cross) and bring out again four threads down. Insert four threads up and four threads to the left then work this half of each cross all along row. On the return journey work second arm of each cross to complete the stitch.

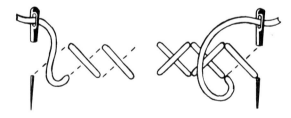

Variations on the basic cross

Double cross Work basic cross stitch then bring needle out four threads down and two vertical threads to the left. Insert needle four threads up and bring out two threads to the left and two horizontal threads down. Complete stitch by inserting needle four threads to the right and bring out two threads down and four threads to the left in readiness for the next stitch.

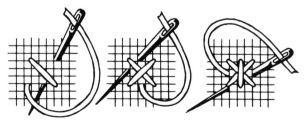

Double straight cross This consists of a straight cross stitch worked over four horizontal and four vertical threads, with a basic cross stitch worked over the centre of the straight cross over two horizontal and two vertical threads.

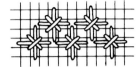

Long-legged cross Work from left to right. Work the second arm over double the number of threads of the other arm – e.g. work the first arm over eight threads, the second over four.

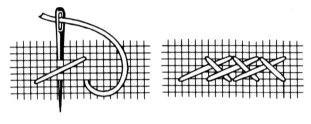

Oblong cross This is an 'oblong' version of the basic cross stitch. Stitches are worked over four horizontal and two vertical threads.

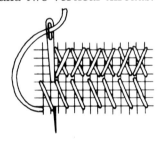

Straight or upright cross This is usually worked over two horizontal and two vertical threads. A straight vertical stitch is crossed by a straight horizontal stitch. Rows of straight cross stitches should be worked between each other to give an interlocked appearance.

See also **rice stitch** (page 70) and **smyrna cross stitch** (page 71).

DRAWN-THREAD WORK

In this type of embroidery, threads are withdrawn from the fabric and then embroidery is worked over the edges of the space of the withdrawn threads. Decorative stitches may also be worked over the loose threads which are left when the

Linen mat with hemstitched insertions.

warp and weft threads are withdrawn. This is one of the easiest and most ancient forms of open-work embroidery, and the foundation of lace. The drawn-thread technique is often used to create a decorative hem.

Basic hemstitch

Measure required depth of hem, plus the turnings and withdraw required number of threads. Do not withdraw the threads right across fabric, but only to form a square or rectangle. Cut threads at the centre and withdraw gradually outwards on each side to within the hem measurement leaving a sufficient length of thread at corners in order to darn the ends invisibly. Turn back the hem to the space of the drawn threads, mitre corners and baste. Bring the working thread out two threads down from the space of drawn threads through the folded hem at right-hand side, pass the needle behind four loose threads, bringing needle out two threads down through all the folds of the hem in readiness for next stitch. The number of threads may be varied to suit the fabric or design.

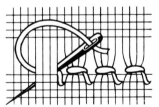

Ladder hemstitch

In this the basic hemstitch is worked along both edges of the spaces of drawn threads.

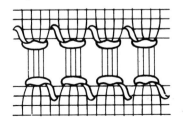

Zigzag hemstitch

This is similar to ladder hemstitch but there must be an even number of threads in each group of loose threads caught together in the first row. In the second row, the groups are divided in half, so that each group is composed of half the number of threads from one group and half from the adjacent group. A half group starts and ends the second row.

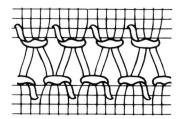

Diamond hemstitch

Withdraw threads from the fabric for the required width, miss six threads and withdraw another band of the same number of threads. Bring needle out four loose threads to the left. Working on band of threads not withdrawn, from right to left, bring needle through four threads to the left and three threads down. Insert needle four threads to the right, bring out at starting point, insert three threads down and bring out four threads to the left. Insert four threads to the right and bring back out four threads to the left. Insert three threads up. Continue in this way to the end of the row, and finish off thread by securing neatly on wrong side of embroidery. Turn fabric and work back along row forming diamond shapes as shown in diagram 2.

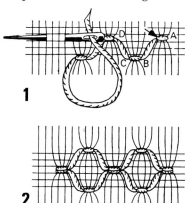

Double (or Italian) hemstitch

Withdraw threads from the fabric for the required width, miss the same number of threads and withdraw another band of the same number of threads. Bring the needle out four (or less) loose threads to the left in the top band of drawn threads, pass the needle behind the four threads, bringing it out where the thread first emerged. Pass the needle down over the fabric

and under four loose threads in the lower band of drawn threads; pass the needle over the same four threads and under the fabric bringing it out four threads to the left in the top band of drawn threads. These two movements are worked throughout. The free edges of the drawn-thread spaces can be hemstitched in the usual way.

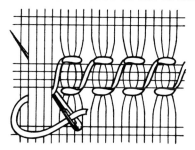

Overcast bars

Withdraw the number of threads required from the fabric and separate the loose threads into bars by overcasting firmly over these threads as many times as necessary to cover the group of threads completely.

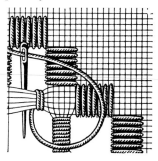

Woven bars

Withdraw an even number of threads from the fabric and separate the loose threads into bars by weaving over and under an even number of threads until the threads are completely covered.

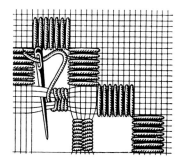

DRAWN-FABRIC WORK

This creates a similar open-work appearance to drawn-thread work, but no threads are withdrawn from the fabric – instead, groups of threads are pulled together by stitching. The actual stitching is not the main feature of the work – it is the open pattern formed on the fabric by the pulling together of the threads. The stitches are worked over a regular number of threads, and the working thread is always pulled firmly with each needle movement so that an open-work effect is achieved. Although drawn-fabric work looks fragile, because no threads are withdrawn the embroidery remains strong and durable. The following are a few drawn-thread stitches.

Four-sided stitch

This stitch is worked from right to left, and can be used as a border or a filling. Bring the needle through at the arrow on diagram 1, insert the needle four threads up, bring it through four threads down and four to the left, insert at starting point and bring out four threads up and four to the left. Insert needle at A on diagram and bring out at B. Continue in this way to the end of the row or close the end for a single four-sided stitch. Turn the fabric round for next and each successive row and work in a similar way. Pull all stitches firmly.

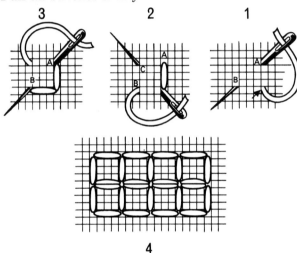

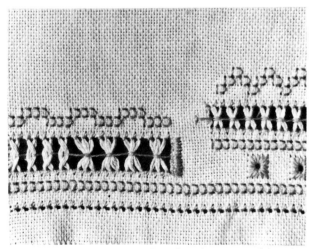

Above and right: samples showing a combination of drawn-thread and drawn-fabric stitches.

Pin stitch

This stitch can also be used in drawn-thread work and for outlining appliqué work. For a hem edge, bring the needle through the folded hem at A on diagram 1, insert the needle at B and bring out at C; insert once more at B and bring out at C. Insert again at B, bring out through the folded hem at D. Continue in this way to the end of the row. Pull all stitches firmly.

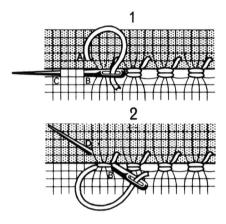

Punch stitch

Work two straight stitches into same place over four threads, then bring the needle out four threads down and four threads to the left in readiness for the next stitch. Work along the row in this way. Turn the fabric for next and each successive row. Diagram 2 shows the squares completed by turning the fabric sideways and working in a similar way.

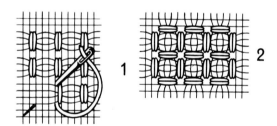

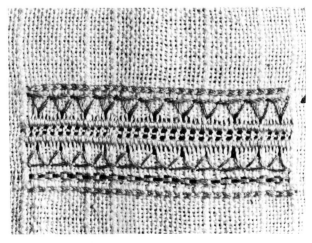

Ringed back stitch

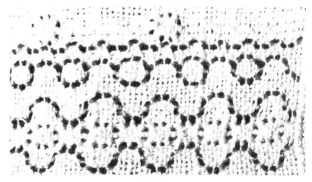

Work from right to left. Bring needle through and insert three threads down, bring it through six threads up and three threads to the left, insert it at starting point, bring it through three threads down and six to the left, insert three threads to the right. Continue working back stitches in this way to make half rings, as shown in diagram. Turn the fabric round for the second row and work in a similar way to complete the rings. All connecting stitches are worked into the same holes.

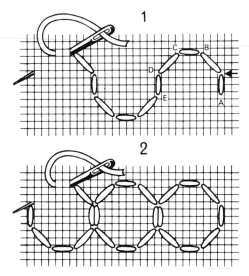

Motif used in traditional Scandinavian embroideries.

Three-sided stitch

Work from right to left. Bring the needle through at A (diagram 1) and take two stitches from A to

B over four threads of the fabric; bring the needle through at A and take two stitches from A to B over four threads of fabric. Bring the needle through at A and take two stitches from A to C (four threads up from A and two to the right). Bring the needle through at D (diagram 2), four threads to the left, take two stitches from D to C, bring the needle through at D. Take two stitches from D to A (diagram 3). Bring the needle through at E (diagram 4), four threads to the left. Diagram 5 shows a corner turning. Pull all stitches firmly.

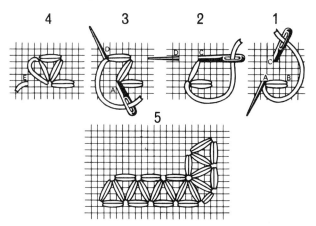

SOME NATIONAL COUNTED-THREAD EMBROIDERY STYLES

Assisi

This is worked in cross and Holbein stitches. It differs from normal cross stitch designs in that the background is stitched, and the pattern motifs left plain. The design is first outlined with Holbein stitch, then the background filled in with cross stitch.

Blackwork

Often known as Spanish blackwork because the embroidery is reputed to have originated in Spain. Traditionally designs are based on floral motifs from Spanish medieval architecture and engravings, and are stitched with black thread on white linen. Stitches used include back stitch, whipped back stitch and cross stitch. Modern blackwork designs can be worked with coloured threads and fabrics, with fairly simple natural forms as pattern motifs.

Hardanger

This embroidery comes from Norway, and is named after the Hardanger Fjord. Traditionally it is worked in white thread on coarse white linen. Satin stitches are worked in groups of an uneven number of stitches. When all the satin stitch blocks are complete, the fabric threads are cut and withdrawn as required. The loose threads are overcast or woven to form bars and various filling stitches worked within the spaces left by the drawn threads. Designs are usually geometric in character.

Hedebo

Hedebo embroidery, worked in white thread on white linen, is a traditional form of Danish needlework, and takes its name from the stretch of heath (*hede*) that lies between Copenhagen and Roskilde. Since time immemorial the peasants who lived there have spun and woven their own linen from the flax grown on their farms, and their pride in their home-made articles was very great. It was a natural development that they should ornament their garments with stitching. The idea of drawing out some of the threads and rearranging them with a needle and thread was their first attempt at Hedebo work. Eventually a beautiful tradition in cut and drawn-work was established. Design motifs are frequently outlined with chain stitch.

Rhodes

Also sometimes known as punch or punched embroidery. This is really drawn-fabric work in reverse, for the background only is worked in drawn-fabric stitches and the pattern motifs left clear. This creates solid shapes against an attractive net-like background.

Roumanian

This, like Assisi work, is worked in cross and Holbein stitches, but here the pattern motifs are in cross stitch, the background is left plain, and little decorative scrolls extending from the cross stitch motifs are worked in Holbein stitch.

An example of a traditional Hardanger design.

THE PATTERNS

Cross stitch apron

illustrated in colour on page 49

MATERIALS

Of Clark's Anchor Stranded Cotton (USA J. & P. Coats Deluxe Six Strand Floss) —1 skein each Carnation 029, Rose Madder 055, Cyclamen 087, Electric Blue 0140, Saxe Blue 0147, Forest Green 0218, Emerald 0227, Buttercup 0295, Terra Cotta 0336, Cinnamon 0371, Snuff Brown 0374, White 0402, and Black 0403. ¾ yd. pale green mediumweight evenweave fabric, with 21 threads to 1 in., 59 in. or 54 in. wide. A Milward 'Gold Seal' tapestry needle No. 24.

STITCHES

Cross; back.

DIAGRAM *(see page 48)*

The diagram gives the complete design, showing the arrangement of the stitches on the threads of the fabric. Each background square on the diagram represents three threads of the fabric.

TO MAKE

Note. Use 3 strands of cotton throughout.

Cut fabric into sections as follows: one piece, 37½ in. by 19 in., for main skirt section; one piece, 19 in. by 6 in., for waistband; two pieces, each 21 in. by 6½ in., for ties; two pieces, each 7½ in. by 6½ in., for pockets.

Mark an 11½-in. square with basting stitches centrally on to skirt section, 4¼ in. from lower edge. Mark the centre of this square both ways with basting stitches. The blank arrows on the diagram should coincide with your basting stitches. Begin embroidery centrally and work design as given in diagram following stitch and colour key. Each cross stitch is worked over three threads of the fabric, thus giving approximately seven crosses to 1 in.

Mark the centre of each pocket piece lengthwise with basting stitches. The large basket of flowers in the lower right-hand corner of the diagram is worked on each pocket. With one short side of fabric facing you, begin embroidery at the lower right-hand corner of the basket, 12 threads to the right of basting stitches and 1 in. from lower edge. Work the complete section of the design, following stitch and colour key.

TO COMPLETE

Press embroidery on the wrong side. Turn back ½-in. hems on short sides of apron skirt, and stitch in place. Turn back a 2-in. hem at lower edge and slipstitch in position. Turn back ½ in. on sides and lower edge of pockets and press; turn back a 1-in. hem along top edge, and slipstitch. Stitch pockets in position to skirt, 5¼ in. from sides and 3½ in. down from upper edge. Run two rows of gathering stitches along top edge of apron, making first row ⅜ in. from edge, and the second row ⅛ in. below this. Turn back ½ in. on short ends of waistband and press. Pull up gathers on skirt to fit waistband for approximately 5 in. at each side, leaving centre section flat. With right sides together, stitch waistband to skirt, ½ in. from edge. Fold waistband in half lengthwise and slipstitch in position on wrong side to line of stitching. Fold tie pieces in half lengthwise and machine stitch long sides and one short end ½ in. from edge. Turn to right side. Pleat raw ends to fit open ends of waistband, insert ties and sew neatly in position. Press.

STITCH AND COLOUR KEY

Cross stitch	Back stitch	
☒	–	Carnation
⊘	–	Rose Madder
⚏	–	Cyclamen
◨	–	Electric Blue
◉	–	Saxe Blue
◎	ꜱ	Forest Green
⊠	ꜱ	Emerald
⊓	–	Buttercup
C	–	Terra Cotta
◪	ꜱ	Cinnamon
⋀	–	Snuff Brown
⊡	–	White
■	ꜱ	Black

Dutch-style apron with cross stitch embroidery – instructions start on page 47.

TO COMPLETE

Fold unworked border of fabric to wrong side of choker along dotted line marked on diagram. Turn in raw edges for $\frac{1}{4}$ in. and slipstitch neatly in place. Sew on press fasteners to fasten choker. Press well.

Cross stitch choker

MATERIALS
One skein stranded embroidery cotton in blue, 1 skein in pink, and 1 skein in black. Piece of white medium-weight square-weave fabric, with 22 double threads to 1 in., measuring $14\frac{1}{2}$ in. by $2\frac{1}{2}$ in. (Hardanger fabric is ideal). A tapestry needle No. 24. Two press fasteners.

MEASUREMENTS
Finished choker measures 14 in. long, 1 in. wide.

STITCH
Cross.

DIAGRAM
The diagram gives one end of the choker, plus one complete repeat of the cross stitch pattern. Each background line on the diagram represents one double thread of the fabric.

TO MAKE
Note. Use 3 strands of cotton throughout.
Mark centre of fabric strip lengthwise with basting stitches. Begin embroidery about $\frac{3}{8}$ in. from one short end, on the central basting stitches, and work section of design as given in the diagram. The arrow on the diagram should coincide with your basting stitches. Each cross stitch is worked over two double threads of the fabric. Work all border design in blue, work motif 1 in blue with central stitch in pink, work motif 2 in blue with the four outside stitches of motif in black. Repeat bracketed section of design 18 times (or until choker is length required). Complete pointed end to correspond with beginning.

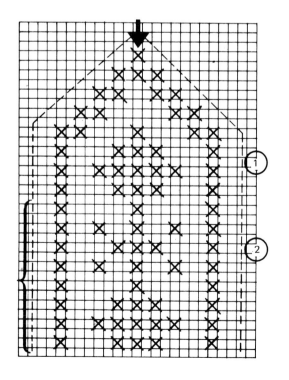

50

Swedish darning trolley set
illustrated in colour on page 52

MATERIALS
To make two trolley cloths: of Clark's Anchor Stranded cotton (J. & P. Coats Deluxe Six Strand Floss) — 3 skeins each Pale Cyclamen 085, Mid Cyclamen 088 and Coffee 0382. ½ yd. jade green fine evenweave fabric, with 25 threads to 1 in., 50 in. wide. A Milward 'Gold Seal' tapestry needle No. 21.

MEASUREMENTS
The finished size of each cloth is 16 in. by 23 in.

STITCH
Darning.

DIAGRAM
The diagram gives a little over half of one motif, showing the arrangement of the darning stitches on the threads of the fabric. The background lines on the diagram represent the threads of the fabric.

TO MAKE
Note. Use 6 strands of cotton throughout.
Cut two pieces from fabric, each 18 in. by 25 in. Mark the centre of each piece of fabric both ways with basting stitches. The black arrows on the diagram should coincide with the basting stitches worked on your fabric. With long side of one piece of fabric facing, commence embroidery centrally, 12 threads to the right and 2 threads down from crossed basting stitches. Work the section of motif given in the diagram, following the colour key. Complete upper half of motif to correspond with section already worked. Repeat complete motif in position shown to the left of crossed basting stitches. Work motif once more on each side. Work other cloth in a similar way.

TO COMPLETE
Press embroidery on the wrong side. Turn in ¾-in. hems, mitre corners and slipstitch. Work a row of running stitches ¾ in. from finished edge over and under two threads of the fabric in coffee shade cotton.

COLOUR KEY
1 Pale Cyclamen
2 Mid Cyclamen
3 Coffee

Swedish darning trolley set – instructions start on previous page.

Austrian cushion

MATERIALS

Of Clark's Anchor Stranded Cotton (USA J. &. P. Coats Deluxe Six Strand Floss) – 2 skeins Flame 0335, 1 skein each Cardinal 019, Lilac 0105, Azure 0154, Mid Almond Green 0261, Dark Almond Green 0263, Buttercup 0293, Terra Cotta 0336, Mid Grey 0400, Dark Grey 0401, White 0402, Black 0403, and Tapestry shade No. 0904 (soft mid brown). ½ yd. pale grey medium-weight evenweave fabric, with 21 threads to 1 in., 54 in. wide. A Milward 'Gold Seal' tapestry needle No. 24. A 16 in. square cushion pad.

MEASUREMENTS

The finished size of cushion is 16 in. square.

STITCHES

Cross; back.

DIAGRAMS *(see page 54)*

Diagram A gives the complete central design, excluding the border, and diagram B gives one quarter of the border design. Both diagrams show the arrangement of the stitches on the threads of the fabric. Each background square represents three threads of the fabric.

TO MAKE

Note. Use 3 strands of cotton throughout.
Cut two pieces from fabric, each 18 in. square. Mark the centre both ways on one piece with basting stitches. The blank arrows on both diagrams should coincide with the basting stitches on your fabric. Begin the embroidery centrally at crossed basting stitches and work design as given in diagram A, following stitch and colour key. Each cross stitch is worked over three threads of the fabric. Work one quarter of the border design, following diagram B and stitch and colour key. Turn fabric and work other three quarters in a similar way.

TO COMPLETE

Press the embroidery on the wrong side. Place the embroidered fabric square against the plain fabric square, right sides facing, and stitch together round three sides taking 1-in. turnings. Trim turnings, and turn right side out. Insert cushion paid, fold in turnings on remaining open edges, and slipstitch neatly together.

STITCH AND COLOUR KEY

Cross stitch	Back stitch		
⊠		–	Cardinal
■		–	Lilac
⊡		–	Azure
	⊓	–	Mid Almond Green
	⊓	–	Dark Almond Green
⃝		–	Buttercup
◣		–	Flame
⬩		–	Terra Cotta
⊡	⊓	–	Mid Grey
◉	⊓	–	Dark Grey
⊔	⊓	–	White
◣		–	Black
⊙	⊓	–	Tapestry Brown

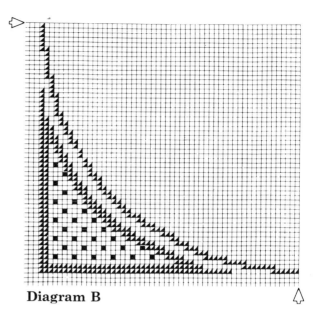

Diagram B

Diagram A

Drawn-thread traycloth

MATERIALS
Of Clark's Anchor Stranded Cotton (USA J. & P. Coats Deluxe Six Strand Floss) — 3 skeins White 0402, 1 skein each Spring Green 0238 and Grass Green 0246. ½ yd. green mediumweight evenweave fabric, with 21 threads to 1 in., 59 in. or 54 in. wide. A Milward 'Gold Seal' tapestry needle No. 24.

MEASUREMENTS
The finished traycloth is 14 in. by 20 in.

STITCHES
Satin; back; diamond hemstitch.

DIAGRAM *(see page 58)*
The diagram gives the right-hand section of the design, showing the arrangement of the stitches on the threads of the fabric. The background lines on the diagram represent the threads of the fabric.

TO MAKE
Note. Use 3 strands of cotton throughout.
Cut a piece from fabric, 18 in. by 24 in. With one narrow end of fabric facing, begin embroidery 2 in. from right-hand side and 3½ in. from lower edge (blank arrow on diagram). Work the section given in the diagram, following stitch and colour key, but omitting diamond hemstitch.

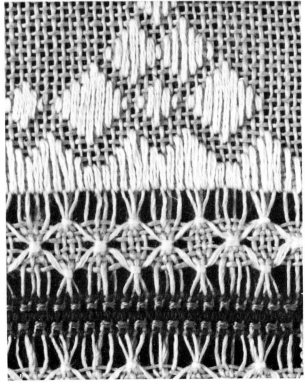

continued on page 58

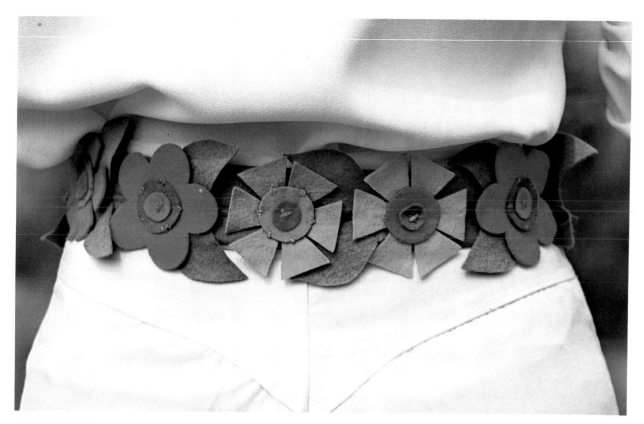

*A pair of embroidered belts. Top picture, above:
flower appliqué belt (see page 131). Lower
picture: heart-patterned needlepoint belt (see
page 74).*

Continue along narrow end of fabric until there are eight points worked in all, finishing to correspond with right-hand side already worked. Cutting from centre of design, withdraw the required number of threads as shown in diagram, each thread being darned separately into fabric at each end of the design. Work diamond hemstitch. Work satin stitch diamond (at top of diagram) nine times on each long side spacing evenly, as shown on diagram. Repeat border design at other narrow end of fabric.

TO COMPLETE
Press embroidery on wrong side. Trim to finished size, plus $\frac{3}{4}$ in. for hems. Turn in hems on all edges, mitre corners and slipstitch.

Cross stitch lunch mats

MATERIALS (to make three mats)
Of Coats Anchor Tapisserie Wool (or any good-quality tapestry wool)—3 skeins Olive Green 0422, and 2 skeins each Light Flame 0332, Mid Flame 0334, and Sage Green 0844. $\frac{1}{2}$ yd. acid yellow mediumweight square-weave cotton fabric, with 6 squares to 1 in., 42 in. wide. A Milward 'Gold Seal' tapestry needle No. 18.

MEASUREMENTS
The finished size of each mat is approximately 16 in. by 12 in.

STITCH
Cross.

DIAGRAM
The diagram gives a little more than half the complete design, showing the arrangement of the stitches on the threads of the fabric. Each background square on the diagram represents one square of the fabric.

TO MAKE
Cut three pieces from fabric, each 18 in. by 14 in. Mark the centre of each piece of fabric both ways with basting stitches. The blank arrows on the diagram should coincide with the basting stitches on your fabric—take care to have the basting positioned exactly as indicated on the diagram. The design is worked throughout in cross stitch, each stitch worked over one square of fabric, thus giving six cross stitches to 1 in. With one long side of one piece of fabric facing, commencing the embroidery centrally and work the given half of the design as in the diagram, following the colour key. Work other half of mat to correspond. Work other two mats in a similar way.

TO COMPLETE
Press embroidery on the wrong side. Trim fabric on each mat to within 9 squares of embroidery at each long side. Turn in $\frac{1}{2}$ in. hems on all edges, and stitch neatly.

STITCH AND COLOUR KEY
1 White   Satin stitch
2 Grass Green   Satin stitch
3 Spring Green   Back stitch
4 White   Diamond hemstitch

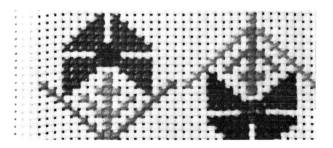

58

COLOUR KEY

⊡	—	Light Flame
◖	—	Mid Flame
⊙	—	Olive Green
◨	—	Sage Green

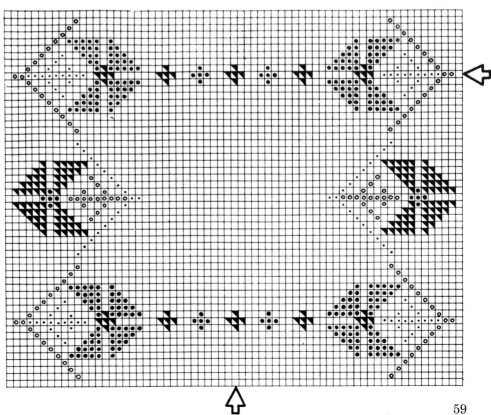

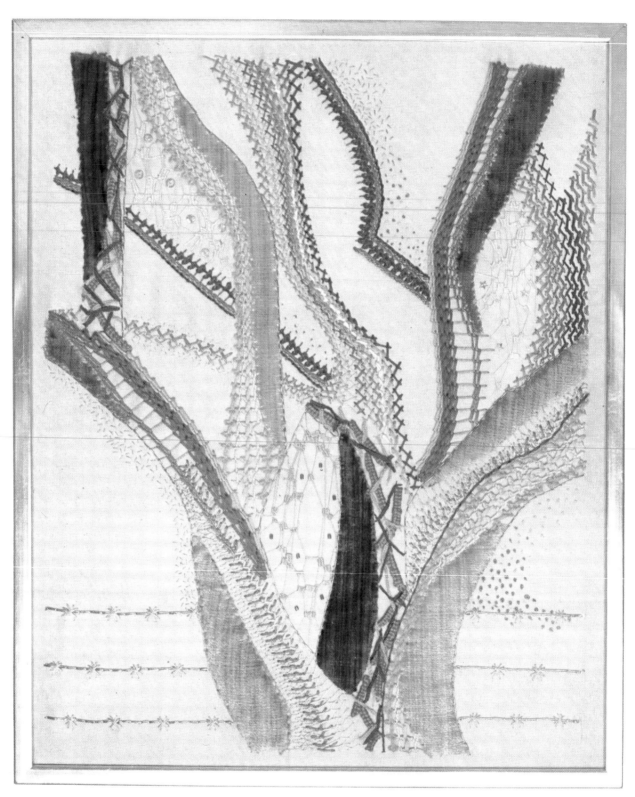

Above: *'Branches', an embroidered picture worked on a gold silk background in wools, soft and stranded cotton, raffia, metal threads and beads, with applied strips of furnishing velvet.*

Opposite: *drawn-fabric runner (see page 62) and Florentine-embroidered cushion (see page 94).*

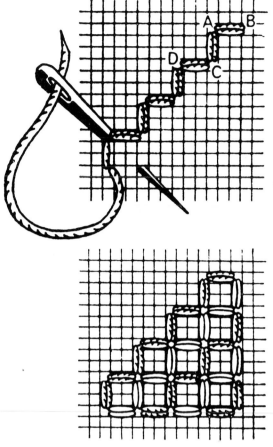

1

2

Drawn-fabric runner

illustrated in colour on page 61

MATERIALS
· 5 skeins Clark's Anchor Stranded Cotton (USA J. & P. Coats Deluxe Sis Strand Floss) in Delphinium 0122. ½ yd. blue mediumweight evenweave fabric, with 21 threads to 1 in., 59 or 54 in. wide. A Milward 'Gold Seal' tapestry needle No. 23.

MEASUREMENTS
The finished size of the runner is 14 in. by 29 in.

STITCHES
Double faggot filling; satin.

DIAGRAMS
Diagram opposite gives a little over half of one motif, showing the arrangement of the stitches on the threads of the fabric. The background lines on the diagram represent the threads of the fabric.

Diagrams, left, show how to work double faggot filling stitch: bring the needle out at A (on Fig. 1), insert at B, bring out at A and insert again at B; bring out at C, insert at A, bring out at C and insert again at A; bring out at D; continue in this way for required number of times. Insert needle as shown in Fig. 1, turn fabric and work second row in a similar way. Turn fabric for each alternate row. Fig. 2 shows the worked corner section, alternate rows shown without shading. Pull each stitch firmly. The stitch may be worked over two fabric threads (as in this design) or over three fabric threads (as shown in Diagram B).

TO MAKE
Note. Use 3 strands of cotton for double faggot filling stitch, 4 strands for remainder of embroidery.

Cut a piece from fabric 16 in. by 31 in. Mark the centre both ways with basting stitches. The black arrows on diagram A should coincide with the basting stitches worked on your fabric. With long side of fabric facing, begin the embroidery with double faggot filling stitch 8 threads to the left of the crossed basting stitches. Work section of the design as given in diagram A, following stitch key. Pull each stitch firmly, with the exception of satin stitch (number 2 on the stitch key). (*Note.* The drawing together of the fabric threads is not shown on the diagram in order to make the counting of the threads and method of working the stitches easier to follow.)

Complete remainder of motif to correspond with first half. Repeat the complete motif four more times on left half of fabric, then turn fabric and work other half in a similar way.

TO COMPLETE
Trim to finished size, plus ¾ in. for hem. Turn in hems on all edges, mitre the corners and slipstitch.

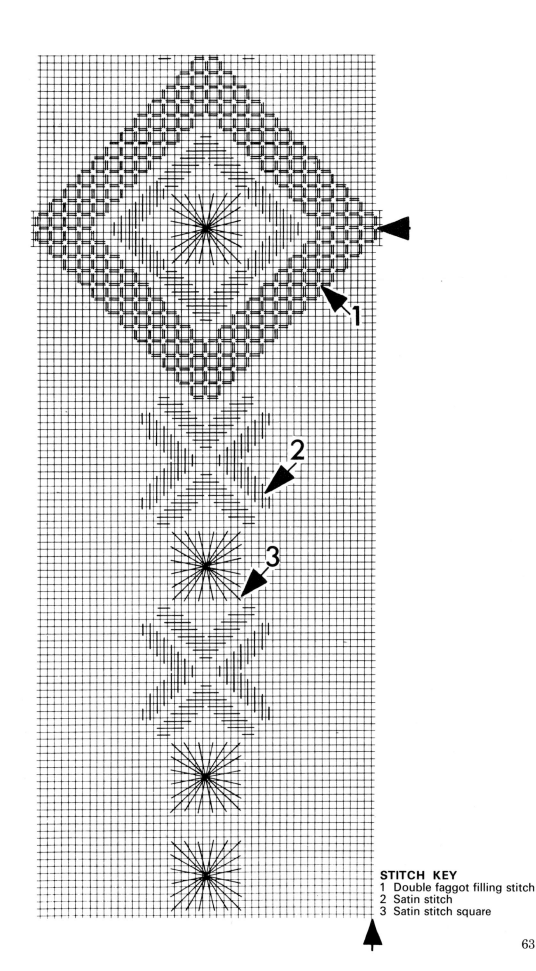

STITCH KEY
1 Double faggot filling stitch
2 Satin stitch
3 Satin stitch square

63

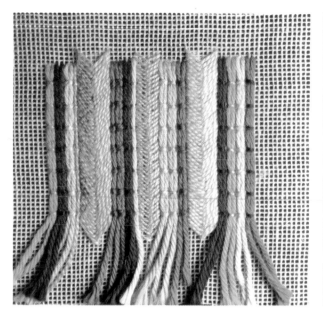

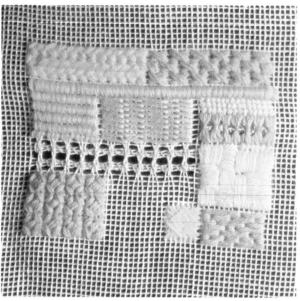

Above: *sample of couching and flat (free embroidery) stitch worked on canvas.*

Above: *sample showing a selection of different needlepoint tapestry stitches.*

Duck panel, worked in an assortment of needlepoint stitches (see page 79).

Chapter three
NEEDLEPOINT TAPESTRY

Needlepoint tapestry is, strictly speaking, not tapestry at all – for the word really means a woven fabric – but is embroidery on a canvas ground. When the embroidery is worked entirely in either tent or gobelin stitch, the effect thus achieved is similar to a woven tapestry, hence the name. But there is a great deal more to needlepoint besides these two traditional stitches: in fact there are dozens of interesting, attractive stitches which can be used, and once an understanding of the craft has been acquired it is possible to invent new stitches. Build up an extensive stitch vocabulary, learn to use threads and colours as an artist uses paints, and you will be able to create all manner of fascinating textures and effects.

EQUIPMENT

The basic equipment for needlepoint tapestry consists of thread, canvas and a frame.

Yarns

Traditionally, only linen, wool and silk threads are used for tapestry work, but in fact a wide range of threads, natural and synthetic, can be most effectively used depending on the type of design being worked.

To begin with, however, stick to the conventional tapestry yarns: tapisserie wool (tapestry wool), crewel wool and stranded embroidery cottons. These are all good hardwearing threads which will withstand the long and constant wear usually demanded by designs made up in needlepoint.

Embroidery cottons and crewel wool can be used in single or multiple strands to suit the canvas mesh: tapisserie wool can only be used in a single strand.

When you become experienced in needlepoint you will no doubt want to experiment with unusual and novelty threads. These can be most successfully used, but whichever yarn you choose to use should never be finer than the threads of the canvas or the background canvas will show through your stitches.

Canvas

Most designs made in needlepoint have to withstand fairly hard wear – for instance, church kneelers, handbags, chair seats, cushions. For this reason, it is important to buy a good-quality canvas. If you work your embroidery correctly, there should be no canvas visible after the design is complete, but nevertheless the choice of a good canvas will give your work a much longer life, and often help to show your stitches to best effect.

Canvas is usually made either from cotton or linen: which you choose is a matter of personal preference, although linen is probably the more hardwearing of the two.

Canvases are available in a choice of double thread or single. In double-thread canvases, the warp and weft threads are arranged in pairs. For a beginner, a single-thread canvas is probably the best choice. Double-thread canvases can be used for detailed designs later where it is wished to use both tent stitch and trammed tent stitch in the same design.

Single and double-thread canvases are made in a range of mesh sizes, to suit different types of designs and different yarns. A wide mesh gives only a few threads or holes to the inch, and is useful for big scale work; a fine mesh has considerably more threads or holes to the inch and should be used for intricate designs.

Canvases are sold by their mesh size: in a single-thread canvas this size is given as the number of threads to the inch; in double-thread canvas this is given by the number of holes to the inch. Mesh sizes usually range from about 10 to 30 threads or holes to the inch, but there are even bigger mesh canvases available, with only 4 or 5 holes to the inch, known as rug canvas.

Needles

The ideal tapestry needle should pass through the canvas easily, without forcing the threads of the canvas apart and without splitting the threads. Sizes of tapestry needles range from 13 through to 24. The lower the number the bigger the needle, so for fine intricate work you would choose a No. 24 needle.

Frames

Many of the stitches used in needlepoint tapestry are diagonal stitches, and if a frame is not used to stretch and control your canvas, then the canvas will be pulled out of shape by the continual slant of stitches in the same direction. There are a number of straight stitches in needlepoint and if you intend to work a design using only these stitches, then a frame will not be necessary.

A round embroidery frame is not suitable for needlepoint work: only use a square or rectangular frame. A simple frame can be easily made by stretching the canvas tautly and pinning it to a wooden picture frame. However there are a number of different types of ready-made frames available if you wish to buy one.

Leader frame This is a simple rectangular frame which has to be supported at a comfortable working height in order to leave your hands free to stitch.

Table frame A self-supported frame which can be placed on a table top. There are usually screw fittings to adjust the frame to give the slant required.

Floor frame Probably the most versatile frame of all. A free-standing, adjustable frame, which can be placed anywhere with work left in position on it.

Travel frame Not recommended for everyday use, but useful if you want to carry your work around, and for small pieces of work. The total depth of this frame is only 12 in., so your work has to be rolled up and re-rolled each time you need a fresh piece of canvas to work on.

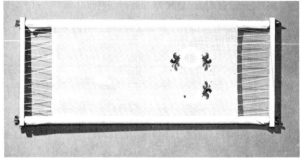

Also useful

Scissors, tape measure, pins and drawing pins, blotting paper for stretching the canvas, waterproof Indian ink for transferring designs to your canvas.

FRAMING-UP CANVAS

Most frames operate on a similar principle: two horizontal, parallel rollers are covered with webbing to which your canvas is attached. The rollers then slot or screw into wooden side struts. The sides of your canvas are laced to these struts.

The width of your canvas should never exceed the length of the webbing on the rollers of the frame.

Before fixing your canvas in position on the frame, you should cut your canvas to size – this should be the size of the finished embroidery plus at least 3 in. extra all round. Mark the centre points horizontally and vertically on your canvas with lines of basting stitches. Make ½-in. turnings at top and bottom edges of canvas, and baste in place. Enclose these and the side edges with a length of 1-in. tape.

Now position canvas on your frame, and stitch top edge of canvas with overcasting stitches to top roller, bottom edge to bottom roller. Finally lace side edges of canvas to side struts of frame, using string or strong button thread. The lacing should be taken through the taped edge of canvas and then round the strut of frame, at regular intervals.

STITCHES

Many of the counted-thread stitches given on pages 41–46 can also successfully be used in needlepoint work, including cross stitch and its many variations. Also, the stitches given for Florentine embroidery (see page 83) are canvas embroidery stitches, so can be incorporated in any needlepoint design.

Brick stitch

This stitch is worked in rows alternately from the left and from the right. It is usually worked over four horizontal threads of the canvas, between alternate pairs of vertical threads. Bring needle through at lower point of each stitch and work stitch upwards. In the following row, stitches are worked in the spaces between stitches of previous row to give an interlocked 'brick' formation.

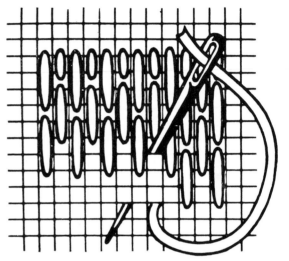

A needlepoint sampler in which many different stitches are combined.

Byzantine stitch

This is a diagonal stitch, worked in 'steps'. Bring needle through canvas and take a stitch four horizontal threads up and four vertical threads to the right. Continue in this way working from bottom right to top left, having six stitches to each step, and working each stitch over four horizontal and four vertical threads.

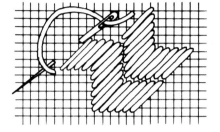

Chequer stitch

Groups of seven diagonal stitches, covering four horizontal and four vertical threads of the canvas, are alternated with groups of sixteen tent stitches also covering four horizontal and four vertical threads.

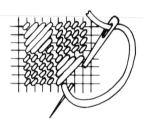

Cross stitch

See page 42 for the basic cross stitch, and its variations. When working cross stitch on canvas, in order to prevent distortion of the canvas, it is essential to complete each cross stitch separately before moving to the next. Work as follows: bring needle out at bottom right point of cross, insert four threads to the left and four threads up at top left point and bring out four threads down. Insert four threads up and four threads to the right.

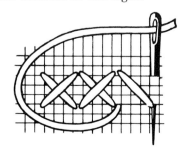

Diagonal stitch

Any stitch worked in a slanting direction across the canvas threads can be termed a diagonal stitch. In its traditional form however, each stitch is worked in turn over two, three, four and then three intersections of the canvas threads. Continue working in this sequence from top left to bottom right. In the following row, work stitches to fit exactly into the zigzag of previous row.

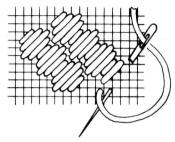

Fern stitch

Work from top to bottom. Bring needle through at top left-hand corner and take a diagonal stitch two vertical threads to the right and two horizontal threads down. Bring needle through one vertical thread to the left. Insert two vertical threads to the right, two horizontal threads up. Bring back out three threads to the left, one thread down. Continue in this way.

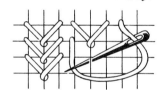

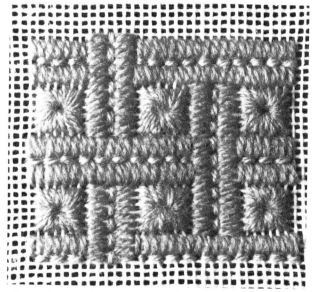

Sample showing eyelets and upright gobelin stitch.

The width of your canvas should never exceed the length of the webbing on the rollers of the frame.

Before fixing your canvas in position on the frame, you should cut your canvas to size – this should be the size of the finished embroidery plus at least 3 in. extra all round. Mark the centre points horizontally and vertically on your canvas with lines of basting stitches. Make ½-in. turnings at top and bottom edges of canvas, and baste in place. Enclose these and the side edges with a length of 1-in. tape.

Now position canvas on your frame, and stitch top edge of canvas with overcasting stitches to top roller, bottom edge to bottom roller. Finally lace side edges of canvas to side struts of frame, using string or strong button thread. The lacing should be taken through the taped edge of canvas and then round the strut of frame, at regular intervals.

STITCHES

Many of the counted-thread stitches given on pages 41–46 can also successfully be used in needlepoint work, including cross stitch and its many variations. Also, the stitches given for Florentine embroidery (see page 83) are canvas embroidery stitches, so can be incorporated in any needlepoint design.

Brick stitch

This stitch is worked in rows alternately from the left and from the right. It is usually worked over four horizontal threads of the canvas, between alternate pairs of vertical threads. Bring needle through at lower point of each stitch and work stitch upwards. In the following row, stitches are worked in the spaces between stitches of previous row to give an interlocked 'brick' formation.

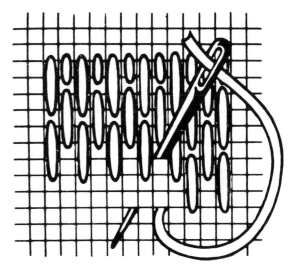

A needlepoint sampler in which many different stitches are combined.

67

Byzantine stitch

This is a diagonal stitch, worked in 'steps'. Bring needle through canvas and take a stitch four horizontal threads up and four vertical threads to the right. Continue in this way working from bottom right to top left, having six stitches to each step, and working each stitch over four horizontal and four vertical threads.

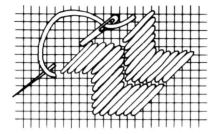

Diagonal stitch

Any stitch worked in a slanting direction across the canvas threads can be termed a diagonal stitch. In its traditional form however, each stitch is worked in turn over two, three, four and then three intersections of the canvas threads. Continue working in this sequence from top left to bottom right. In the following row, work stitches to fit exactly into the zigzag of previous row.

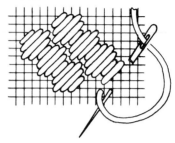

Chequer stitch

Groups of seven diagonal stitches, covering four horizontal and four vertical threads of the canvas, are alternated with groups of sixteen tent stitches also covering four horizontal and four vertical threads.

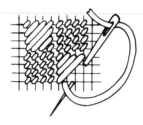

Fern stitch

Work from top to bottom. Bring needle through at top left-hand corner and take a diagonal stitch two vertical threads to the right and two horizontal threads down. Bring needle through one vertical thread to the left. Insert two vertical threads to the right, two horizontal threads up. Bring back out three threads to the left, one thread down. Continue in this way.

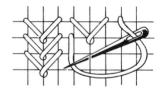

Cross stitch

See page 42 for the basic cross stitch, and its variations. When working cross stitch on canvas, in order to prevent distortion of the canvas, it is essential to complete each cross stitch separately before moving to the next. Work as follows: bring needle out at bottom right point of cross, insert four threads to the left and four threads up at top left point and bring out four threads down. Insert four threads up and four threads to the right.

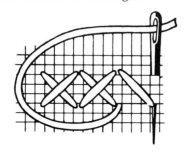

Sample showing eyelets and upright gobelin stitch.

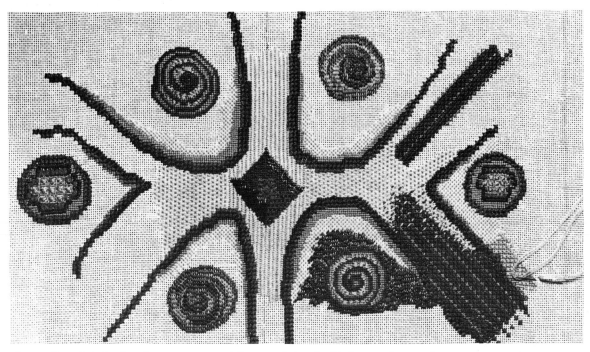

A needlepoint design in progress, with a variety of stitches and yarn types.

Flat stitch

This is worked in blocks of diagonal stitches, each block consisting of five stitches and covering three horizontal threads and three vertical threads. Blocks of stitches slant alternately to the left and to the right.

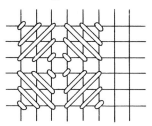

Gobelin stitch

Work in rows alternately from the left and from the right. In the first row, worked from left to right, work diagonal stitches across one vertical thread to the left and two horizontal threads down. Bring needle out two horizontal threads up and two vertical threads to the right. In the following row, needle is inserted from above downwards instead of upwards from below to give the same slant of stitch. See also **straight gobelin stitch** (page 86).

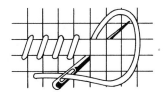

Half cross stitch

This is simply the first half of the complete basic cross stitch. It may be worked from left to right, or right to left.

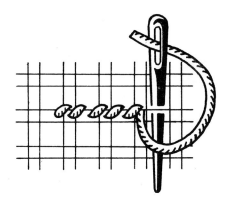

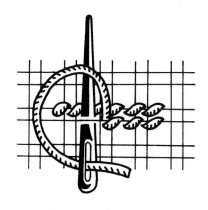

Sample using knitting yarn and pearl cotton.

Jacquard stitch

This, like Byzantine stitch, is worked in diagonal rows from bottom right to top left, in steps of six stitches each. Rows of diagonal stitches worked over two horizontal and two vertical threads, are alternated with rows of tent stitch.

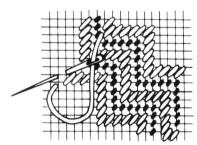

Knotted stitch

Work a diagonal stitch over three horizontal and one vertical threads, then work a small horizontal stitch over the centre of the diagonal stitch to tie it down. Work in rows, overlapping each row by one thread of the canvas.

  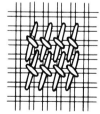

Parisian stitch

This is similar to Hungarian stitch (see page 86) and often confused with it. Work upright stitches alternately over one and then three horizontal

threads. In the following row, stitches are worked in alternate sequence from the previous one so they interlock.

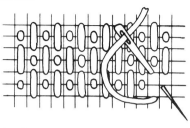

Rice stitch

In this a basic cross stitch is worked over four horizontal and four vertical threads, then a small straight stitch is worked over each corner of the basic cross. It is usual to work the crossed corner stitches in a contrasting yarn and colour to the basic cross.

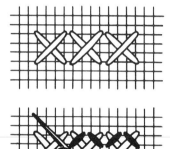

Satin stitch

This is a simple straight stitch, which may be horizontal or vertical, worked from right to left, or left to right, and over any number of threads as required.

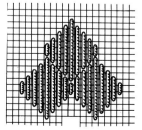

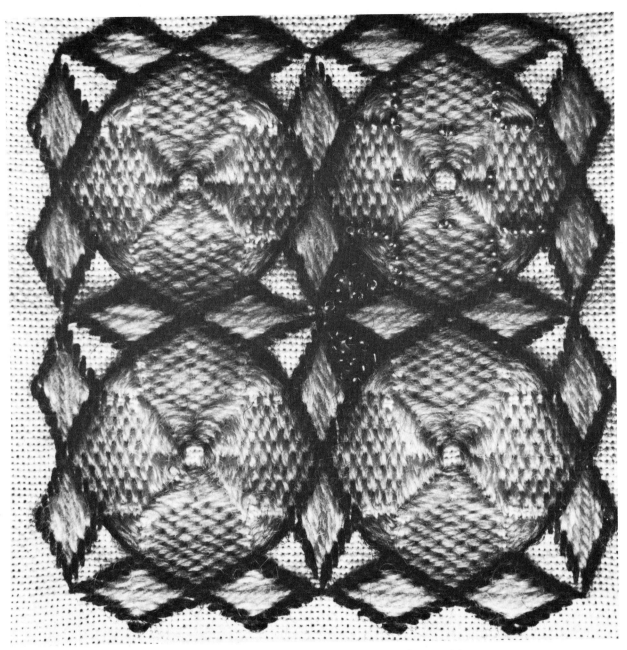

A Victorian needlepoint design, with tiny beads worked in with the stitching.

Scottish stitch

Blocks of five diagonal stitches covering three horizontal and three vertical threads of the canvas, are outlined with tent stitches, each worked over a single intersection of canvas threads.

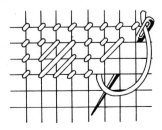

Smyrna cross stitch

Work a basic cross with a straight cross over it. A smyrna cross is usually worked over four by four threads.

Tent stitch

Sometimes known as petit point stitch. It may be worked over single canvas, or if worked over double-thread canvas then the threads are opened up so each tent stitch is worked over a single intersection. Bring the needle out on the left-hand side of area where stitching is to appear on the top part of the first stitch. Pass the needle down over one horizontal thread and one vertical thread to the left. Bring it out one horizontal thread up and two vertical threads to the right. Continue in this way. In the following row, worked from right to left, the needle passes the crossed threads up and over, then under two threads. All stitches should slope in the same direction.

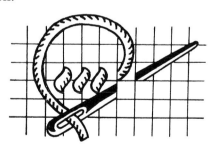

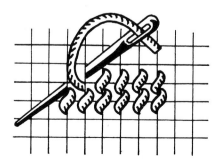

Trammed tent stitch

This form of tent stitch gives a denser coverage to the canvas, and a richer appearance to your finished design. It must be worked on double-thread canvas. The stitch is sometimes known as gros point stitch. Bring needle through at a point where a pair of vertical threads cross a pair of horizontal threads, then take a straight horizontal stitch across work (the stitch should not be longer than five inches) from left to right. Pull needle through just below and to the left of the intersection. Work a tent stitch over the double-thread intersection of canvas threads and pull needle through on the lower line two double threads (vertical) to the left in readiness for the next stitch. Work tent stitches across the trammed stitch in this way, then bring needle out between a crossing of canvas threads on the line below and work another trammed stitch from left to right. Work tent stitches from right to left over this, as before. Continue in this way.

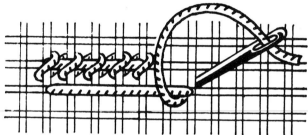

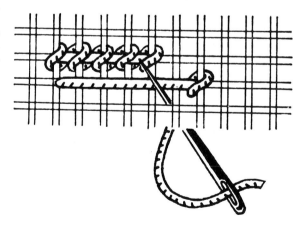

Trammed stitch, split

If it is wished to give dense coverage to your canvas work split trammed stitches over the canvas and then work the finished embroidery stitches over this tramming. Tramming should be worked in a similar colour and thread as the finished design. Bring needle through at a point where a pair of vertical threads of the canvas cross a pair of horizontal threads. Insert needle the required distance along (no longer than five inches) and bring through the canvas at a similar crossing of threads. Bring needle through one vertical thread to the left on the same line, through the stitch just made, thus forming a split stitch. Continue in this way.

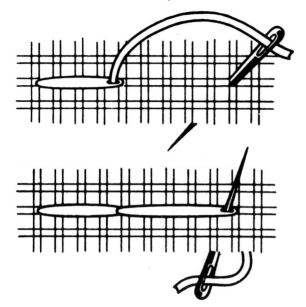

STRETCHING CANVAS

After your embroidery is complete, before making it up into the required finished item, the canvas should be stretched. This will compensate for any distortion caused by the pull of the stitches. Stretch the canvas in the following way: cover a flat wooden surface with a few sheets of damp blotting paper, and using a sponge soaked in cold water, thoroughly dampen the back of the embroidered canvas. Place canvas right side up, on the board over the damp blotting paper and using drawing pins carefully pin the canvas to the board, pinning the top edge first, then pulling opposite edge taut and pinning it. Pin side edges in a similar way. Canvas must be left until thoroughly dry and this can take up to two or even three weeks, depending on the weight of the canvas and threads. When canvas is completely dry, unpin from board and make up into finished article.

QUICK HINTS TO HELP

Never work with a thread longer than about sixteen inches as the constant friction of canvas against thread can fray it away in places.

If on completion of a design you find several small patches of canvas showing through, disguise these by working tent stitch or any suitable small stitch over the area.

It is normal to start in the centre of a design and work outwards. However, leaving the whole of the background area until last can be tedious.

It is therefore permissible to have several parts of a design being worked at the same time. Leave needles and threads in position ready for you to continue with whichever part of the design appeals to you at a particular time.

Try to keep the tension of your stitches even. It should be neither too loose nor too tight. Yarn should fill each hole of the canvas, and the stitches must cover the canvas completely and bed evenly together to form a smooth texture.

If your canvas is correctly stretched on the frame it is impossible to make any stitch in one movement: with right hand on top, insert the needle downwards through the canvas and pull the needle through with the left hand. With the left hand, push the needle upwards through the canvas and pull the needle up and out with the right hand.

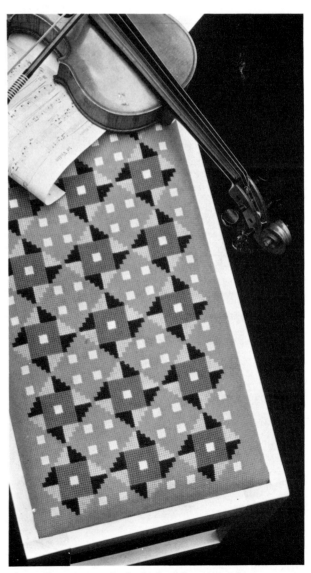

A modern tent stitch design for a stool top.

THE PATTERNS

Heart-patterned belt
illustrated in colour on pages 56 and 57

MATERIALS
3 skeins tapestry wool in cream, 3 skeins crewel wool in dark blue, 2 skeins crewel wool in medium blue, 3 skeins crewel wool in red, and 1 skein stranded cotton in pink. Piece of single-thread tapestry canvas, with 14 threads to 1 in., to measure $8\frac{1}{2}$ in. wide, and the length of your waist size plus 12 in. A $2\frac{1}{2}$-in. buckle. Strip of belt backing to measure $3\frac{1}{2}$ in. wide, and the length of your waist size plus 7 in. A tapestry needle No. 18.

MEASUREMENTS
Finished belt should be the size of your waist plus 6 in. for ease of fit and buckle overlap; $2\frac{1}{2}$ in. wide.

STITCHES
Cross; straight gobelin (see page 86); back; straight cross; satin; tent; smyrna cross; Parisian; Hungarian (see page 86); double straight cross.

DIAGRAMS
Diagram A gives the pointed end of belt, the cross stitch border, one dividing bar, and the first heart panel.
Diagram B gives the second heart panel. **Diagram C** gives the third heart panel.
Each diagram shows the position of the various stitches, and the background lines represent the threads of the canvas.

TO MAKE
Mark centre of canvas lengthwise with basting stitches. Prepare canvas and frame-up.
Begin embroidery on the central basting stitches 3 in. down from one short end of canvas. Work the pointed tip of belt, the dividing bar and the first heart panel, as given in diagram A, first. The arrow on this diagram should coincide with your basting stitches. When the first heart panel is completed work another dividing bar followed by the second heart panel (diagram B), then work another dividing bar followed by the third heart panel (diagram C). Continue in this way working heart panels in rotation, always separating each with a dividing bar, and continuing double row of cross stitches down each side of work to form border. Continue until embroidery measures your waist size plus 6 in. (or length required).
Use threads and colours as follows, using 4 strands of crewel wool and 3 strands of cotton throughout (except for centre of first heart panel).

Border: dark blue crewel wool, cross stitches, each stitch worked over two horizontal and two vertical threads of the canvas.
Dividing bars: centre row of bar is worked in dark blue crewel wool, straight satin stitches worked in blocks of five horizontal stitches, four vertical stitches alternately, each block covering four horizontal, four vertical threads of the canvas. On either side of this centre row is worked a row of cross stitches in medium blue crewel wool, each stitch over four horizontal and four vertical threads of the canvas. Small back stitches are worked on either side of each cross, and between crosses, as indicated on diagram A.
Backgrounds: all worked in cream tapestry wool; in straight gobelin stitch, each stitch over two threads of the canvas, and arranged in alternate interlocking pattern, for first heart panel background; in Hungarian stitch, over four and two threads of the canvas, for second heart panel background; in Parisian stitch, over four and two threads of the canvas, for third heart panel background, and also background for pointed end section of belt.
First heart panel: heart is worked in red crewel wool in straight cross stitch, over two horizontal, two vertical threads of the canvas, with a centre section worked in six strands of pink stranded cotton in tent stitch.
Second heart panel: heart is worked in smyrna cross stitch, with red crewel wool for basic cross, pink stranded cotton for straight cross. Each complete stitch covers four horizontal, four vertical threads of the canvas.
Third heart panel: heart is worked in double straight cross stitch in red crewel wool, over four horizontal, four vertical threads of the canvas.

TO COMPLETE
Stretch canvas if necessary. Trim canvas to within 1 in. of embroidery. Press the unworked borders to back of belt and baste to hold in position. Take short straight end of belt over bar of buckle and baste. Cut one short end of backing fabric to pointed shape to match embroidery, plus $\frac{1}{2}$ in. for seam allowance. Turn in $\frac{1}{2}$-in. seam allowance round all edges of backing and place on embroidered strip, wrong sides together. Oversew neatly round edges.

STITCH KEY

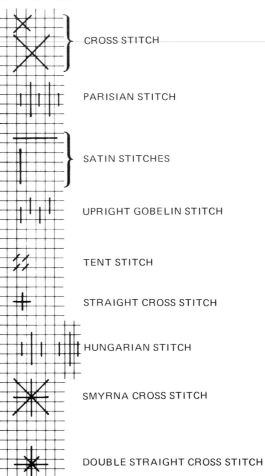

CROSS STITCH

PARISIAN STITCH

SATIN STITCHES

UPRIGHT GOBELIN STITCH

TENT STITCH

STRAIGHT CROSS STITCH

HUNGARIAN STITCH

SMYRNA CROSS STITCH

DOUBLE STRAIGHT CROSS STITCH

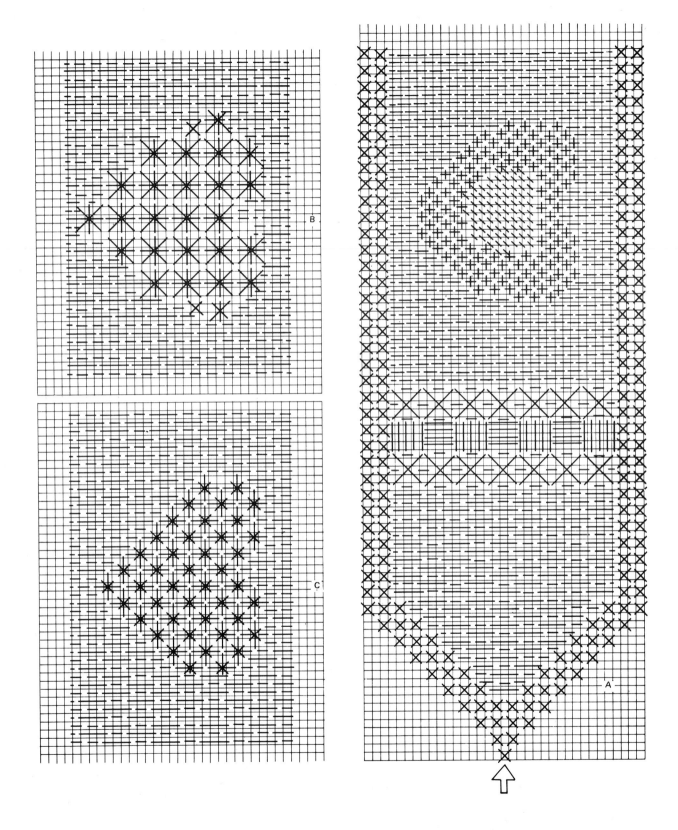

Chair seat

MATERIALS
Of Coats Anchor Tapisserie Wool (or any good-quality tapestry wool) – 14 skeins Light Grey 0397, 12 skeins Olive Green 0423, 6 skeins each Canary Yellow 0288, and Amber Gold 0308, and 1 skein White 0402. ¾ yd. double-thread tapestry canvas, with 10 holes to 1 in., 27 in. wide. A Milward 'Gold Seal' tapestry needle No. 18. A chair with an inset seat pad measuring 18½ in. long, 19½ in. wide at front edge, 16½ in. wide at back edge. Upholstery tacks or nails.

MEASUREMENTS
Finished chair seat measures approximately 18½ in. long, 19½ in. wide at front edge, and 16½ in. wide at back edge.

STITCH
Trammed tent.

DIAGRAMS
Diagram A gives a section of the complete design (one complete hexagonal motif). Each background square on the diagram represents the double threads of the canvas. **Diagram B** (see page 78) gives just over half the design showing the arrangement of the hexagonal motifs.

TO MAKE
Mark the centre of the canvas both ways with basting stitches, run between a pair of narrow double threads lengthwise and widthwise. Mark out total area of embroidery to fit seat pad. Prepare canvas and frame-up. Begin embroidery centrally and work the section given on diagram A, following colour key. The design is worked throughout in trammed tent stitch. The blank arrows on diagram A should coincide with your basting stitches. Following diagram B for position of hexagonal motifs in relation to each other, complete one half of the complete design; the broken lines on diagram B indicate the centre, and should coincide with your basting stitches. Work other half of design to correspond.

TO COMPLETE
Stretch canvas if necessary. Place the embroidery right side up centrally on the chair pad, fold back the unworked border of canvas and secure in position on the underside with tacks or nails.

COLOUR KEY

◙	–	Canary Yellow
⊠	–	Amber Gold
⊡	–	Light Grey
☐	–	White
◪	–	Olive Green

Diagram A

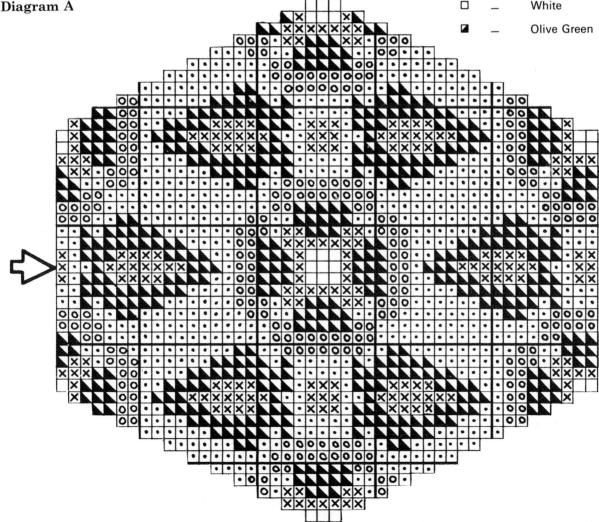

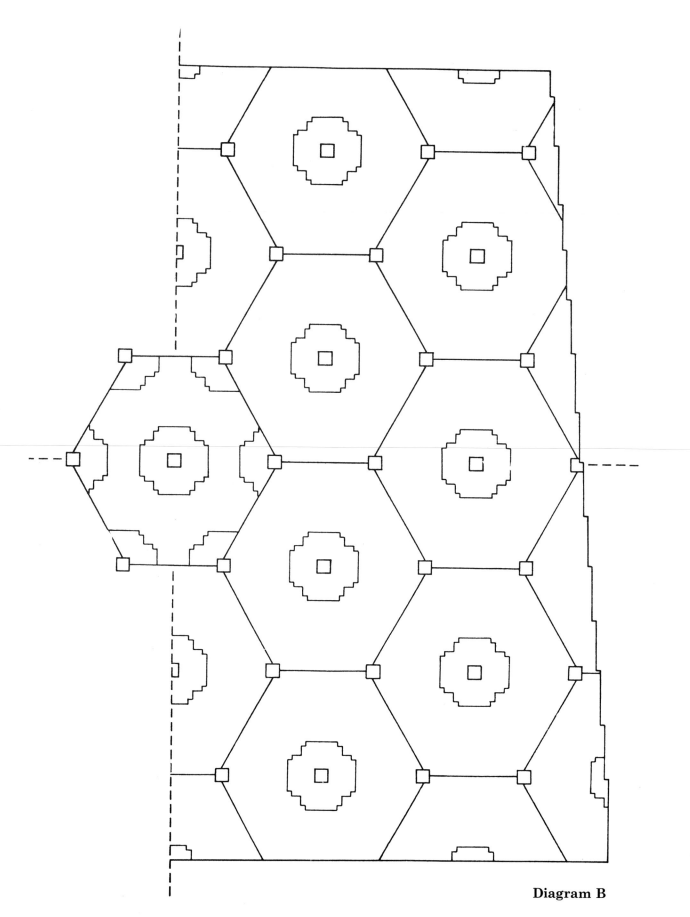

Diagram B

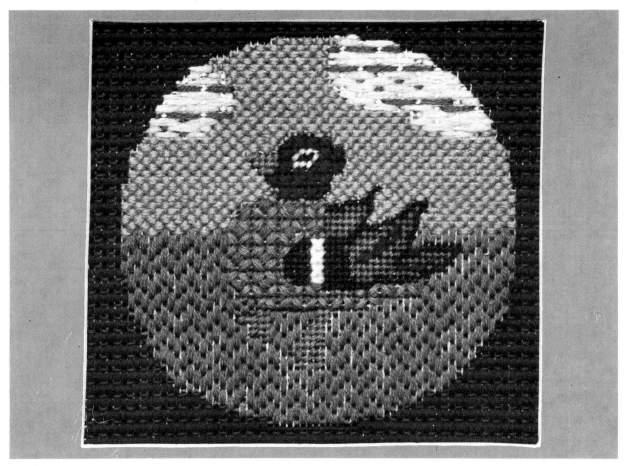

Duck panel *(illustrated in colour on page 64)*

This is worked on single-thread tapestry canvas, with 10 threads to 1 in., in a variety of stitches. The finished embroidery measures 6½ in. by 7 in., so in order to have a 3-in. border of unworked canvas round embroidery you will need a piece measuring 12½ in. by 13 in. The design is mainly worked in crewel wool, with a little stranded cotton. Use a tapestry needle No. 18.

Background: this is worked in red crewel wool, in trammed straight gobelin stitch. Use three strands of wool for tramming, four of wool for stitches, and take each stitch over two threads of the canvas. Work back stitches between the rows of gobelin stitches with red stranded cotton.

Sky: four strands of pale blue crewel wool, straight cross stitch, each stitch worked over two horizontal, two vertical threads of the canvas.

Clouds: three strands of crewel wool in white and mid blue, horizontal darning stitches over five threads of the canvas. Small single stitches worked in three strands of white stranded cotton between darning stitches.

Water: four strands of mid blue crewel wool, Florentine stitch in 3:1 step, with three stitches to each 'wave' (see page 83).

Duck: head in four strands of red crewel wool, cross stitch over two by two canvas threads; eye in white and blue crewel wool (four strands), tent stitch; beak and feet in yellow crewel wool (four strands), tent stitch; body in two shades of grey crewel wool (four strands), rice stitch, over four by four canvas threads; wings are in two shades of grey crewel wool (four strands), tent stitch, with a vertical line of white cross stitches, over two by two canvas threads, and a few diagonal and

straight stitches in red crewel wool to highlight wing and tail.
Mount picture on card, and frame it, if wished.

Stool top

(illustrated in colour on page 81)

MATERIALS

Of Coats Anchor Tapisserie Wool (or any good-quality tapestry wool) — 20 skeins Peacock Blue 0170, 10 skeins Muscat Green 0281, 5 skeins White 0402, 3 skeins Mid Blue 0168, and 2 skeins Pale Blue 0158. ⅝ yd. double-thread tapestry canvas, with 10 holes to 1 in., 27 in. wide. A Milward 'Gold Seal' tapestry needle No. 18. A stool with inset pad measuring approximately 23½ in. by 15 in. Upholstery tacks or nails.

MEASUREMENTS

The finished stool top measures 23½ in. by 15 in.

STITCH

Trammed tent.

DIAGRAM *(see page 80)*

The diagram gives half the design. Each background square on the diagram represents the double threads of the canvas.

TO MAKE

Mark the centre of the canvas both ways with basting stitches, run between a pair of narrow double threads lengthwise and widthwise. Mark out total area of embroidery to fit stool pad. Prepare canvas and frame-up. With one long side of canvas facing you, begin embroidery centrally and work the half given in the diagram, following colour key. The design is worked throughout in trammed tent stitch. The blank arrows on the diagram should coincide with your basting stitches. To complete the embroidery, turn the diagram and work other half in a similar way.

TO COMPLETE
Stretch canvas if necessary. Place the embroidery right side up centrally on the stool pad, fold back the unworked border of canvas and secure in position on the underside with tacks or nails.

COLOUR KEY

◨	–	Pale Blue
◉	–	Mid Blue
⊡	–	Peacock Blue
◪	–	Muscat Green
☐	–	White

Stool top in trammed tent stitch – instructions start on page 79.

Chapter four
FLORENTINE EMBROIDERY

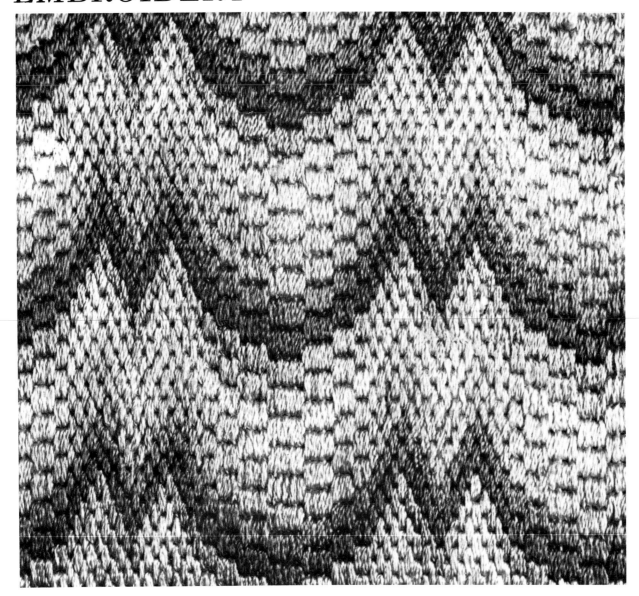

This is a traditional form of canvas embroidery (needlepoint) which can also be worked on even-weave linen. The technique is sometimes incorrectly called Bargello work, because there are some fine examples of Florentine embroidery to be seen in the Bargello Museum, Florence. The technique also includes Hungarian point, fianna or flame stitch. The latter name is derived from the flame-like points which occur frequently in a number of the patterns.

The origin of this style of embroidery is difficult to place, but it is believed to have been brought to Italy by a Hungarian who married one of the Medici family in the 15th century. It was popular in England during the 16th century, and recently has enjoyed a revived popularity both in Great Britain and the USA. Originally it was used to cover entire surfaces including stool tops and chair seats, and so added richness of texture and colour to the upholstery. Nowadays, it can be used in all manner of ways – for fashion accessories such as day and evening bags, for belts and spectacle cases, and for household linen either as border patterns, or allover designs.

Florentine work, probably more than any other embroidery technique, makes marvellous use of colour. The basic principle of a Florentine design is to create a 'wave' or zigzag pattern of upright stitches, each line of stitching worked in a different colour. Traditionally graduated shades of the same colour are used, but in modern designs totally different colours can be used for each row. Colours can also change within rows.

In its simplest form, each step of the zigzag is formed by taking an upright vertical stitch over four horizontal threads of the canvas, and 'stepping' this stitch two horizontal threads above or below the previous stitch (see diagram and detailed instructions below). This is referred to as Florentine stitch in the 4:2 step. Alternatively, a 6:3 stepped zigzag can be worked, by taking each stitch over six horizontal threads, and stepping it three threads above or below the previous one.

Variations on this basic zigzag are endless: try varying the lengths of the individual stitches, the number of stitches worked in each step, and vary the depth of the wave itself – and you will create entirely new patterns. Curves can also be produced in this way, as well as the sharp traditional zigzag form. Usually Florentine patterns tend to be abstract, their interest lying in the vivid and dramatic use of colour, but the patterns can be representative as well – flowers, foliage and birds can all be 'drawn' in Florentine embroidery, once the principles of the techniques have been learned and understood.

Hungarian stitch is frequently combined with Florentine stitch (see below), and so are many other upright needlepoint stitches – e.g. brick and satin. These are useful for filling in areas of canvas which might otherwise be left unstitched when the main Florentine design is completed. As with all canvas embroideries, it is essential that the canvas is completely and smoothly covered by stitching.

MATERIALS

It is usual to work Florentine embroidery on single-thread canvas. Any size mesh, from 14 threads to 28 threads to the inch, may be used, although for first efforts a fairly coarse mesh will be easier to work with. An evenweave linen may, if preferred, be used (see note on evenweave fabrics on page 40).

Whichever type of canvas or fabric you choose, it is essential to choose the right yarn – with canvas, particularly, the yarn used should never be finer than the threads of the canvas mesh, and should fill each hole exactly, so the mesh of the canvas is completely covered in the finished design. Stranded cotton, tapestry or knitting wool, crewel wool and silk, are all suitable yarns. Novelty yarns – such as plastic raffia and metal threads – can also be used to good effect in a modern Florentine design. But experiment with a small sample first of all to see if the yarn suits your canvas, and is reasonably easy to work with. When working designs with a great number of colours, it is a good idea to keep a separate needle ready threaded with each colour.

As with other forms of canvas embroidery, needles should be chosen to suit canvas and thread (see page 65).

As all the stitches used in Florentine work are straight stitches, and there is therefore little danger of canvas distortion, it is not necessary to use a frame. To support a large piece of work as you stitch, roll down the canvas from the top as far as the part of the canvas you are working on. When you stop working, always roll up the canvas carefully. Never fold it.

STITCHES
The basic Florentine stitch

This stitch is usually worked in rows of different colours, to form an allover wave pattern. Stitches are straight and vertical, and can be worked over any number of canvas threads. They are stepped as shown in the diagram, below, to give a zigzag, or wave, of desired depth; the size of the wave may also be varied. A common version of the stitch is to work each vertical stitch over four horizontal threads, stepping each stitch up or down two threads at a time. This is known as the 4:2 step. Each row is an exact repetition of the previous one, so stitches fit together.

 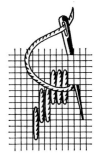

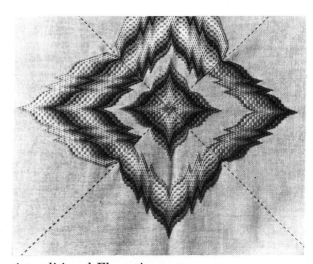

A traditional Florentine pattern.

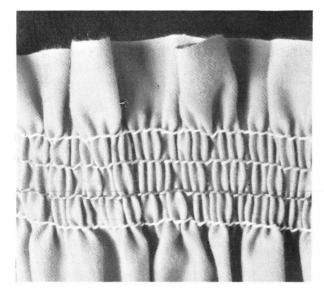

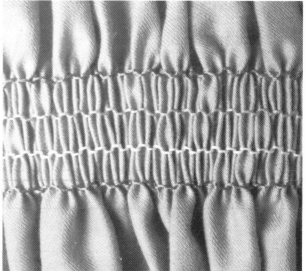

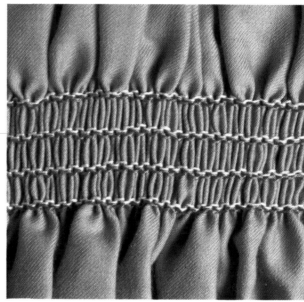

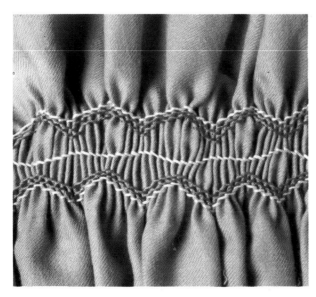

*Traditional smocking stitches (see page 100).
Top row, left to right: outline stitch; cable
stitch. Second row, left to right: double cable
stitch; trellis stitch. Left: three rows of wave
stitch, followed by a row of outline stitch,
followed by another three-row band of wave
stitch, with colours in reverse order to the
first band. Opposite: a sample showing how a
variety of different stitches can be effectively
combined in the same piece of work (see page 100
for working instructions).*

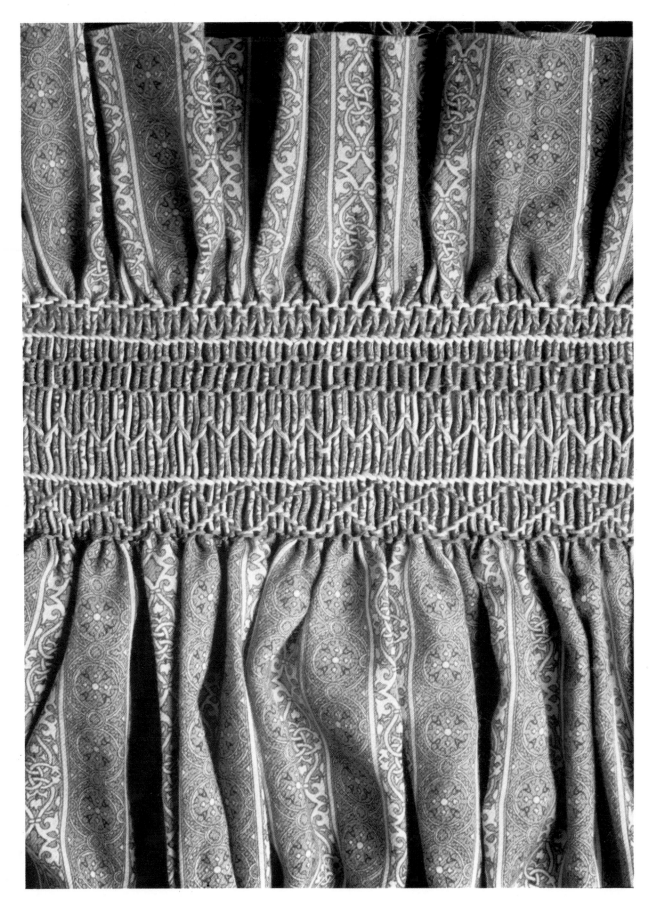

Florentine pattern worked in the 6:1 step.

Hungarian stitch

This is worked in groups of three vertical stitches, each worked in turn over two, four and two horizontal threads; two vertical threads are left between each group, so stitches in the following row can be worked to give an interlocked pattern.

Hungarian ground

This is often used as a background filling in Florentine designs. Rows of basic Florentine stitches, worked in a 4:2 step, three stitches to each wave, are alternated with a row of small upright stitches. Each upright stitch is worked over two horizontal threads, and stitches are arranged in groups of four to form 'diamonds' fitting exactly between the rows of Florentine stitches.

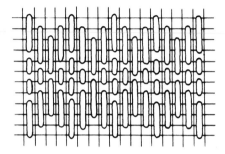

Straight gobelin

This is a useful stitch for filling in unstitched areas at the edges of the canvas. It consists of straight vertical stitches worked over two horizontal threads of the canvas. Work from right to left, or left to right. The stitch may also be worked in an alternate interlocking arrangement, similar to brick stitch (see page 67).

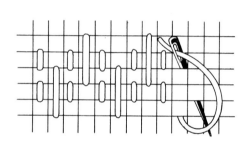

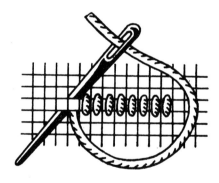

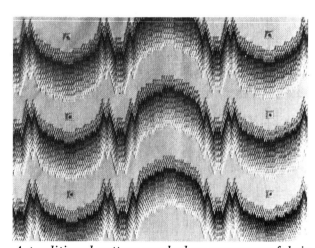

A traditional pattern worked on evenweave fabric.

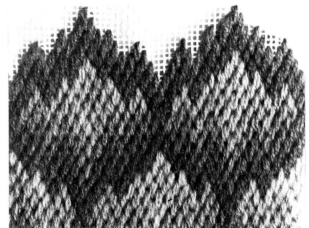

A motif pattern worked in the 4:2 step.

SOME TRADITIONAL FLORENTINE PATTERNS

illustrated on pages 88 and 89

The illustrated samples – with the exception of the basketweave pattern – have been worked on a single-thread canvas with a mesh size of 18 threads to the inch, with two strands of crewel wool, and a No. 24 needle. Where a design is accompanied by a chart, this will indicate the position and length of each stitch on the canvas. The background lines on the chart represent the threads of the canvas.

It is recommended that some of these 'sampler' patterns are worked first to help you become familiar with the Florentine technique, before trying the designs to make beginning on page 91.

Sample 1

This is worked in five shades of blue, the same length stitch is used throughout, and the same step (the 4:2 step – i.e. each stitch worked over four threads of the canvas, stepped up or down by two threads each time), but there is a variable number of stitches in each step. Chart 1 below shows one row of the pattern, indicating the grouping of stitches, and the depth of the wave. Every row is worked alike, to fit into the previous row. Colours range from palest blue (1) through in numerical order to very dark blue (5). Work in the following colour sequence: a row in 5,

followed by rows each in 4, 3, 2, 1, 2, 3 and 4. Continue to repeat this sequence to length required.

Sample 2

This is similar to sample 1 for this is also worked in the 4:2 step, with a variable number of stitches in each step, but the different arrangement of the stitches, the shallower wave, and the change of colours in each row, create an entirely new pattern. Each row is worked exactly as chart 2 below. Four shades of orange are used, three shades of green. Work in the following colour sequence (low numbers indicate lightest shades, high numbers dark shades): 1st row – orange 4; 2nd row – green 3 (first step only), orange 3 (seven steps), green 3 (last step); 3rd row – green 2 (first step), green 3 (second step), orange 2 (five steps), green 3 (one step), green 2 (last step); 4th row – green 1 (first step), green 2 (one step), green 3 (one step), orange 1 (three steps), green 3 (one step), green 2 (one step), green 1 (last step); 5th row – green 1 (two steps), green 2 (one step), green 3 (one step), orange 1 (one step), green 3 (one step), green 2 (one step), green 1 (two steps). As you work this pattern you will see two distinct motifs are formed – a circular motif from the shades of orange, and a smaller diamond motif of greens. Although each row is worked alike in the same sequence of stitches and steps, because of the colour changes within each row, you may find it easier to mark out the positions of the motifs on your canvas, then work in blocks of colour rather than complete rows.

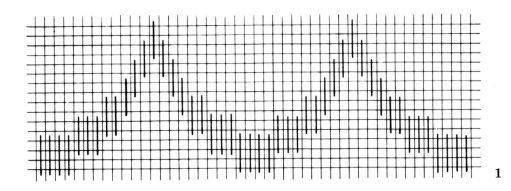

1

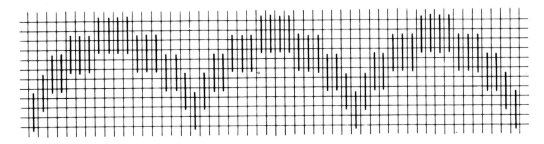

2

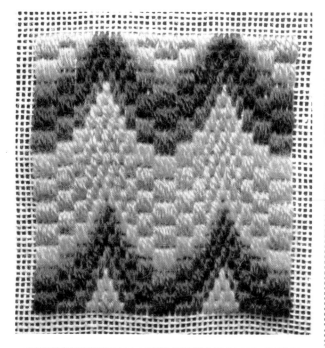

Traditional Florentine patterns (see pages 87, 90 and 91). Top row, left to right: samples 1 and 2. Second line, left to right: samples 3 and 5. Left: sample 4. Opposite: samples 6, 7 and 8 (the three illustrations down left-hand side of page) and sample 9, a traditional honeycomb pattern.

Sample 3

A sharper 'step', variable number of stitches in each step, and a steep wave, creates this angular zigzag pattern. Worked in the 6:1 step (i.e. each stitch is worked over six threads of the canvas, and each step overlaps previous step by only one thread each time), a block of stitches is worked at the base of each wave, then single stitches step up to top of wave. Each row is worked exactly as chart 4 below. Using four shades of purple and one of duck egg blue, work in the following colour sequence, one colour for each row: blue, purple 1, purple 2, purple 3, purple 4.

Sample 4

This shows another version of the pattern type given in sample 2. Again, by changing colours within each row, a distinct circular motif is formed, with diamonds between (only half diamonds are shown on our worked sample). This time, however, the wave (which creates the curve of the circle) is wider, and the circle has a symmetrical arrangement of colours. Each row is worked exactly as chart 3 below. Colours range from cream in centre of circle, through pale peach, mid peach to brown on outside of circle, and from cream at outside of diamond, through pale peach to mid peach in centre of diamond.

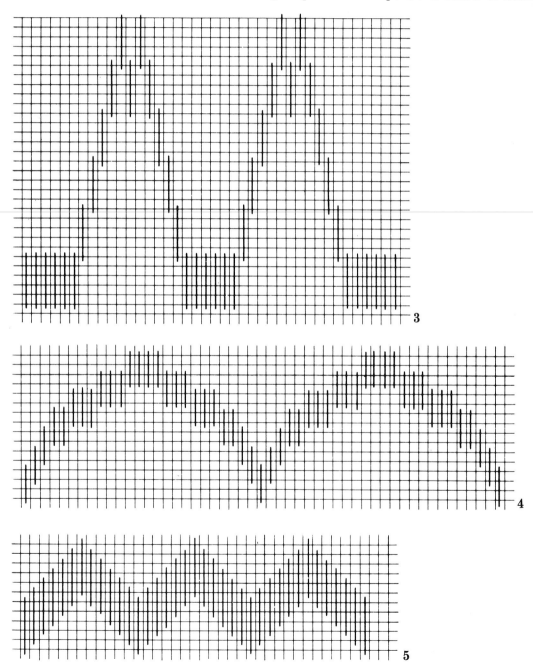

3

4

5

90

Sample 5

Chart 5 is a very regular pattern, with single stitches in the 6:5 step, seven steps to each wave, but by using four shades in each of two different colours, and changing colours within each row, an extremely effective colour pattern is created.

Samples 6, 7 and 8

These three patterns are all worked in the basic 4:2 Florentine step, but show how by altering the depth of each wave, and the colours used within each row, totally different patterns are created.

Sample 9

This is an example of the traditional basketweave pattern. The sample shown is worked on a single-thread canvas with a mesh of 24 threads to the inch. The pattern is worked in the basic 4:2 step, with two stitches to each step, eight steps to each wave. A very clever variation of colours in each row creates this intricate-looking 'plaid' pattern.

THE PATTERNS

Trolley set
illustrated in colour on page 92

MATERIALS (for two trolley cloths, four napkin rings)
Of Clark's Anchor Stranded Cotton (USA J. & P. Coats Deluxe Six Strand Floss) — 6 skeins each Mid Lilac 0105, and Dark Lilac 0106, 5 skeins each Violet 0102, and Parma Violet 0108, 4 skeins each Mid Magenta 062, Dark Magenta 064, and Old Rose 074. ¾ yd. blue mediumweight evenweight linen, with 21 threads to 1 in., 54 or 59 in. wide. A Milward 'Gold Seal' tapestry needle No. 21. ⅛ yd. interfacing, 32 or 36 in. wide. Eight press fasteners.

MEASUREMENTS
The finished size of each trolley cloth is 18 in. by 24 in.; of each napkin ring 2½ in. by 7½ in.

STITCH
Florentine: worked in basic 4:2 step, with a variable number of stitches in each step.

COLOUR KEY

- Mid Magenta
- Dark Magenta
- Old Rose
- Violet
- Mid Lilac
- Dark Lilac
- Parma Violet

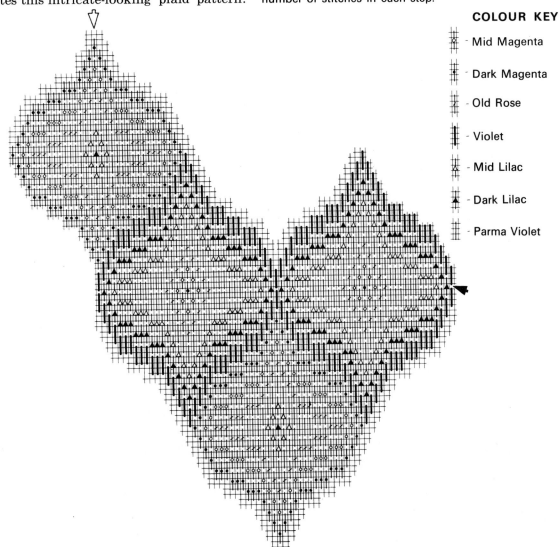

DIAGRAM *(see previous page)*
The diagram gives a section of the design, showing the arrangement of the stitches on the threads of the fabric. The background lines on the diagram represent the threads of the fabric.

TO MAKE
Note. Use 6 strands of cotton throughout.
Cut two pieces from fabric, each 19½ in. by 25½ in., for the trolley cloths, and four pieces, each 6½ in. by 9 in., for the napkin rings. Mark large pieces across the centre

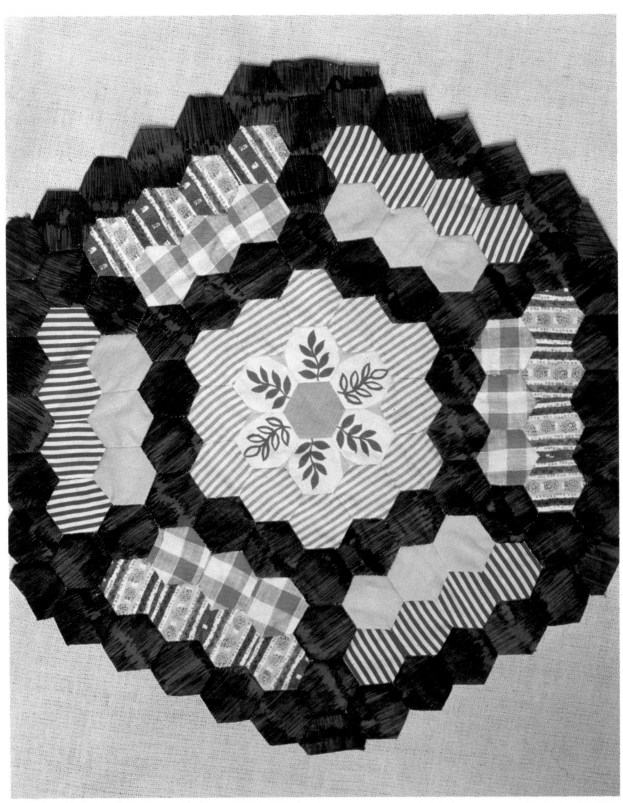

Cushion cover worked in honeycomb patchwork. (see page 107). The hexagon patches are cut from plain and patterned cotton fabrics, and groups of patterned patches arranged to create separate design shapes. The dark green patches form a background framework for the pattern.

both ways with basting stitches. Mark small pieces across the centre lengthwise with basting stitches.

Trolley cloth

With one short side of fabric facing you, begin embroidery centrally 93 threads down from crossed basting stitches, and work section of design as given in the diagram. The blank arrow on the diagram should coincide with your lengthwise basting stitches. Each stitch is worked over four threads of the fabric; follow the colour key for thread colours. Repeat section once more to the right, then work left-hand side to correspond. Turn fabric and repeat on opposite short side.

Napkin ring

With one long side of fabric facing you, begin embroidery centrally at black arrow on diagram, $\frac{3}{4}$ in. in from right-hand side of fabric, and work four motifs along basting stitches.

TO COMPLETE

Press embroidery on the wrong side. Turn back and stitch $\frac{1}{2}$-in. hems on all edges of trolley cloths, mitre corners and slipstitch.

Cut four pieces from interfacing, each $2\frac{1}{2}$ in. by $7\frac{1}{2}$ in. Place an interfacing strip centrally on to wrong side of each napkin ring embroidery. Turn back seam allowance at short sides and stitch lightly to interfacing. Fold long sides towards centre, and slipstitch together. Slipstitch ends. Sew two press fasteners to each napkin ring to fasten.

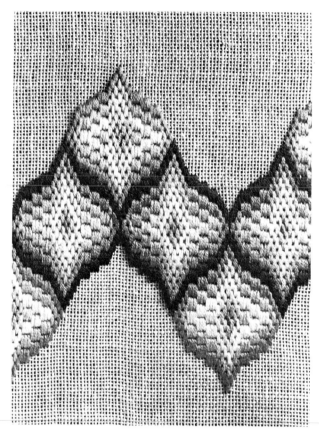

Cushion

illustrated in colour on page 61

MATERIALS

Of Coats Anchor Tapisserie Wool (or any good-quality tapestry wool) – 11 skeins Dark Moss Green 0269, 1 skein each Pale Blue 0158, Medium Blue 0161, Dark Blue 0162, Navy Blue 0164, Medium Moss Green 0266, Light Muscat Green 0278, Medium Muscat Green 0280, Dark Muscat Green 0281, and White 0402. $\frac{1}{2}$ yd. single-thread tapestry canvas, with 18 threads to 1 in., 23 in. wide. $\frac{1}{2}$ yd. dark green velvet or similar mediumweight fabric, 36 in. wide, for backing. 2 yd. matching cord, approximately $\frac{1}{4}$ in. thick, for edging. A Milward 'Gold Seal' tapestry needle No. 19. A cushion pad 16 in. by 12 in.

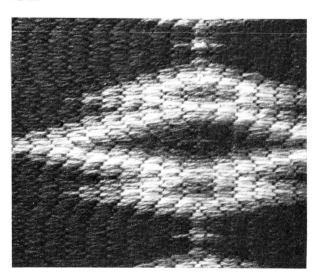

MEASUREMENTS

Finished size of cushion is approximately 16 in. by 12 in.

STITCH

Florentine: worked in 6:1 step, a single stitch to each step.

DIAGRAM

The diagram gives a section of one quarter of the design motif, plus a section of background area, showing the arrangement of the stitches on the threads of the fabric. The background lines on the diagram represent the threads of the fabric.

TO MAKE

Mark the centre of the canvas both ways with basting stitches. Mark out total area of embroidery to fit cushion pad. Prepare canvas.

Begin the embroidery centrally at crossed basting stitches, and work the section of design as given in the diagram. The blank arrows on the diagram should coincide with your basting stitches. Each stitch is worked over six threads of the fabric; follow the colour key for thread colours. Work bracketed section on diagram once more to the right. This completes one quarter of the design motif. Work other three quarters of the design motif to correspond, then extend the background stitches on all sides to the required size.

TO COMPLETE

Trim canvas to within 1 in. of embroidery. Cut a piece of similar size from the backing fabric. Place fabric and embroidered canvas together, right sides facing, and sew round three sides. Turn right side out. Insert cushion pad. Turn in seam allowances on the remaining open edges and slipstitch together. Sew cord round cushion edges, making a loop at each corner.

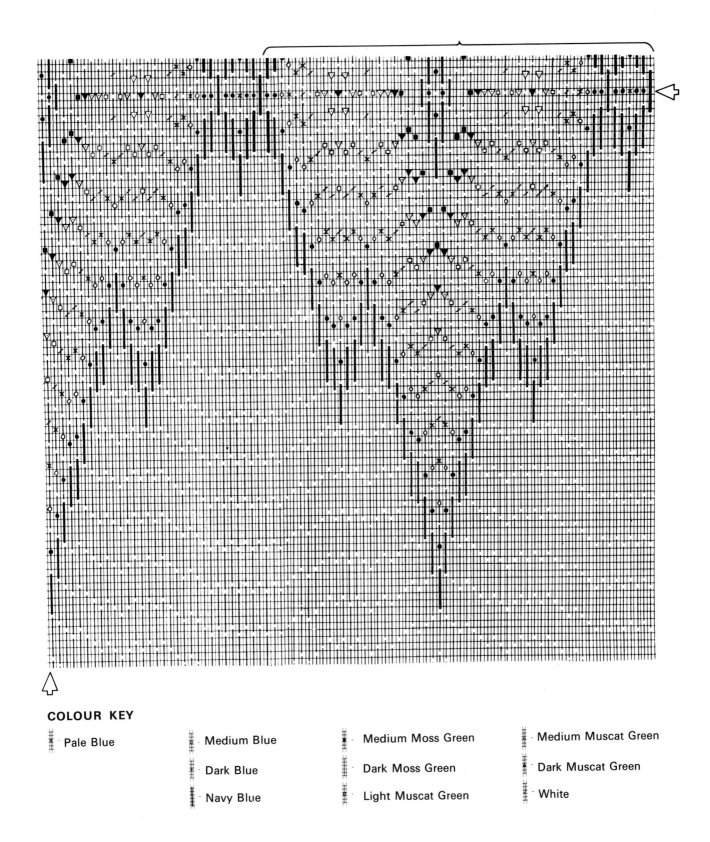

COLOUR KEY

Pale Blue	Medium Blue	Medium Moss Green	Medium Muscat Green
	Dark Blue	Dark Moss Green	Dark Muscat Green
	Navy Blue	Light Muscat Green	White

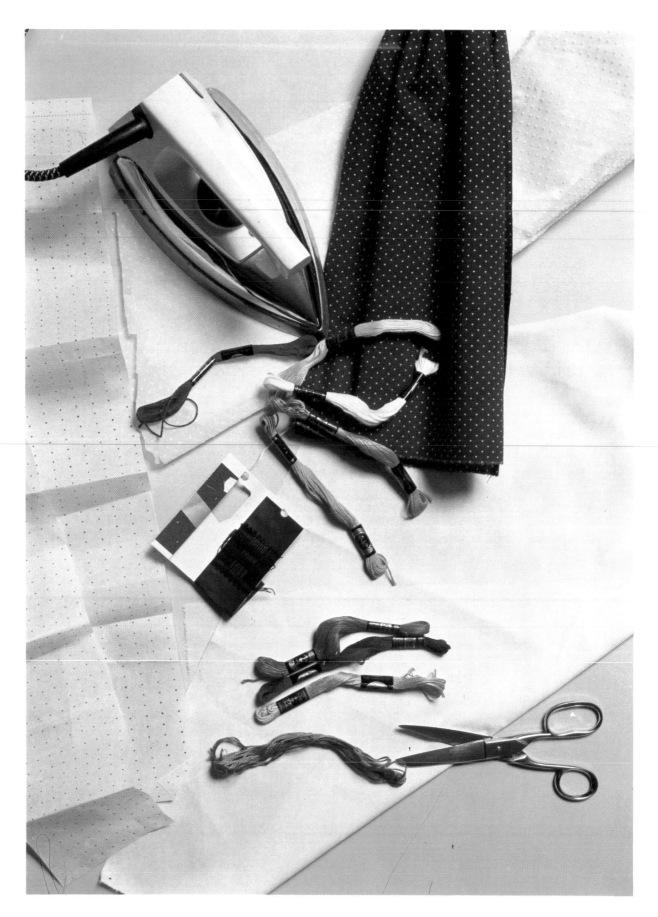

Chapter five
SMOCKING

Smocking was devised as 'a kind of needlework for holding gathers in place' and was originally used on the shiftlike garments worn by shepherds and agricultural workers. These 'smocks' were usually made of linen or homespun hemp, and they were rather like an elongated shirt or nightshirt. The gathers allowed freedom of movement without the garment looking too shapeless.

Apart from the embroidery which held the gathers in place, the smock was usually decorated on the yoke, collar and side to denote the occupation of the wearer. Thus gardeners would have flowers and leaves; shepherds had crooks, hurdles and sheep; wagoners and carters had cartwheels, whip lashes and reins; milkmaids had churns and butter pats; even gravediggers' smocks were decorated – usually with crosses!

Different districts had different coloured smocks, and some can still be seen today in museums. Usually the Sunday-best smock was in white or natural linen, worked in a self colour.

Nowadays smocking is used on all sorts of fabrics and for many types of garments: frocks, nightdresses and rompers for babies; party dresses for little girls; nightdresses and blouses for adults; cotton dresses for teenagers.

FABRICS AND THREADS

Almost any type of fabric can be smocked, such as voile, nylon, organza, lawn, fine cotton, poplin, silk, shantung, crêpe-de-chine, lingerie fabrics, gingham, and fine woollen fabrics. Heavier weights, such as linen, velvet and medium-weight woollen fabrics, can also be smocked successfully, but textured fabrics do not gather well. So choose your fabric according to the garment you wish to make.

If you are using a plain-coloured fabric, a smocking transfer will be needed to help you draw up the work evenly (these can be obtained from most needlework shops and good department stores). Many spotted, striped and checked fabrics can be drawn up without the use of a transfer, as the pattern on the fabric can be used as a guide. As smocking reduces the width of the fabric to approximately one third of its original size you will have to allow for this in your calculations when buying fabric.

The thread normally used for the embroidery is six-stranded embroidery cotton as this can be split to suit the weight of the fabric to be smocked. Two strands are used for light fabrics such as voile, nylon and organza, three strands for medium fabrics such as cotton and fine wools, and four strands for heavier fabrics like velvet or wool. Silk thread can be used to smock silk, shantung or crêpe-de-chine, and it is traditional to use linen thread to smock linen. Never use wool as this is too heavy and breaks too easily.

Colour depends on personal preference, but a very bright-coloured fabric such as scarlet looks most attractive smocked all in white. Pastel and white fabrics look effective smocked in a self colour or in a soft range of muted toning colours; patterned fabrics look best if the smocking complements the colours in the patterns.

PREPARING THE FABRIC

As smocking is worked on gathered fabric, it is essential the fabric is carefully and thoroughly prepared. The gathers must be uniform, and if the work is to have the necessary elasticity, the gathers should be made in the ratio of approximately $2\frac{1}{2}$:1 so allow at least two-and-a-half inches of fabric for every inch of finished smocking.

If you are working with plain fabric you will need to apply a smocking transfer first. This is like a normal embroidery transfer, but it consists only of rows of evenly-spaced dots, printed in blue or yellow. The yellow shows up well on dark fabrics – the blue is better for light-coloured fabrics. Select the size of transfer to suit your work – the larger the garment and heavier the fabric, the more widely spaced the dots should be.

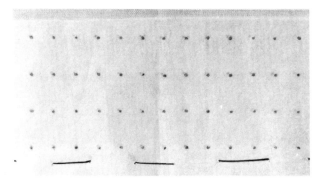

It may be necessary to cut a portion of the transfer off if it is too wide or deep for your fabric, or you may have to add on an extra piece.

The dots are transferred on to the *wrong* side of the fabric, and the work is gathered on the *wrong* side, then the smocking is worked on the gathers on the *right* side of the fabric. First, press the fabric, according to type, then position the transfer on your material – allow for seams and do not place it too near the selvedge (the work is gathered from selvedge to selvedge across the width of the fabric). Make sure the dots are in line with the weave of the material, then baste the transfer in position along the top. Iron over the transfer with a warm iron, or a cool one if the fabric is very delicate, or a synthetic. Then remove the transfer. If your fabric is spotted, checked or striped you may not need the transfer and the fabric can be drawn up by counting out regular points on the pattern, however it may have to be gathered up on the right side if the design is not printed on both sides of the fabric.

Having transferred the dots and removed the transfer, start gathering up the work. Use a strong thread of a suitable weight for the fabric and a separate length for each line of gathering. It is easier if you use a colour which contrasts with your fabric. Each dot *must* be picked up in the needle. Start at the right-hand side with a knot and a back stitch to make it secure, then put the needle in one side of every dot and bring it out at the other, carry the thread to the next dot

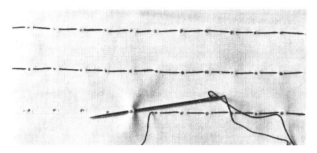

and continue to the end of the row, taking care you put the needle in each side of the dot and not through the middle. Leave the thread loose at the left-hand side. When all the lines have been threaded with the running thread, pull up the work carefully to the required width. If you are making very deep gathers, pull up a few at a time. Tie the loose ends of the gathering threads in

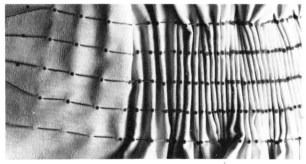

pairs, or if you prefer, the loose ends may be secured by twisting them round pins. Turn the work to the right side and even out the gathers. The gathering threads are never removed until all the work is complete.

The fabric is now ready to be smocked on the *right* side, unless it is likely to fray badly. If so, machine stitch or whip raw edges by hand first. Before starting to smock, plan the design carefully; a true sense of balance between the different types of stitches should be maintained. Try to avoid monotony by interspersing straight stitches with those which form a diamond pattern and do not overcrowd the work – never be afraid to leave a blank line here and there. Do not pull the smocking stitches too tightly when working the design, otherwise you will close up the pleats and lose the elasticity.

STITCHES

Cable stitch

Secure threads on first pleat at left-hand side. This stitch is worked over two pleats by catching up one pleat with the needle, the thread being alternately above and below the needle.

Chevron stitch

This is sometimes known as **baby wave stitch,** when worked in a single row, or **baby diamond stitch,** when worked as two rows to form a diamond pattern.

Work from left to right, as shown in diagram 1. Begin with needle to the left of first pleat. Take stitch straight across first and second pleats, with thread below needle. Bring needle out to left of second pleat, above stitch just made. Keeping thread below needle, take next stitch across third pleat but insert needle on gathering line above. Bring needle out to left of third pleat. With thread above needle, stitch over third and fourth pleats, bringing needle out to left of fourth pleat, below stitch. Now take thread back down to lower line and stitch across fifth pleat, bring needle out to the left of it. Continue in this way. Diagram 2 shows a second row of chevron stitch worked in reverse to form a diamond pattern.

1

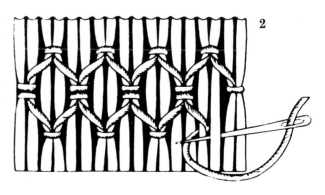

2

Double cable stitch

Work two rows of cable stitch close together, but for each stitch on the first row where the thread was above the needle work stitch immediately below it, on the second row, with the thread below the needle. Similarly for each stitch on the first row where the thread was below the needle, work the stitch below with the thread above the needle.

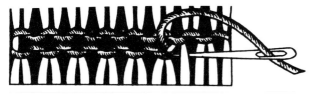

Honeycomb stitch

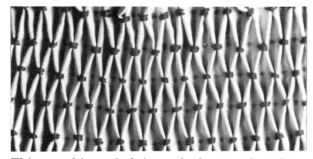

This smocking stitch is used where gathers have to be held together, but a definite design is not required. It also differs from other smocking stitches in that most of the thread is hidden in the folds of the fabric, and in fact only shows at the point where gathers are drawn together. Other smocking stitches are worked on the surface of the gathers. Traditionally, honeycomb stitch is worked with thread just a shade lighter or darker than the fabric, but it looks equally effective worked with a boldly contrasting thread – white fabric, for instance, looks attractive smocked with red thread, or cream fabric with orange. To work honeycomb stitch, bring needle through at the top line of first pleat and work a back stitch over it and second pleat, drawing them together. Work a second back stitch, then take needle down at the back of the second pleat to the lower line of gathering threads, bring it

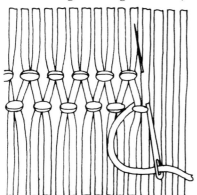

through and work another double back stitch this time over second and third pleats. Take needle up at the back of the third pleat to upper line and work a double back stitch over third and fourth pleats. Continue in this way. Always have the thread above the needle for the top level stitch, and below the needle for lower level stitch.

Mock chain stitch

This consists of one row of outline stitch worked close to one row of stem stitch to form a chain-like effect.

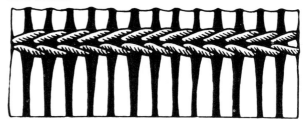

Outline stitch

Secure thread at left-hand side of work, and bring the needle through to the left of the first pleat. Pick up top of the next pleat, inserting the needle with a slight slant and having the thread above the needle. Continue in this way.

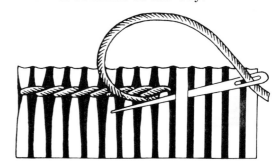

Stem stitch

Work from left to right, with the thread over two folds of fabric, but pick up only the top of one fold with the thread always kept below the needle.

Surface honeycomb stitch

This is sometimes known as **turret** or **vandyke stitch.** Bring the needle through on first pleat at lower level. Draw the needle horizontally through the second pleat keeping the thread below the needle. With the thread still below,

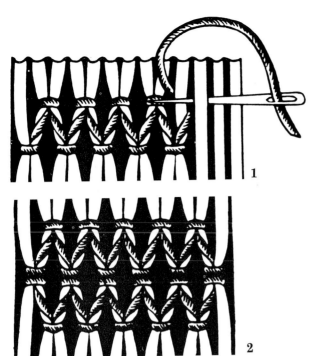

1

2

insert the needle horizontally through the same pleat on top level. With the thread above the needle, insert horizontally through third pleat on top level, and still with thread above, insert the needle through the same pleat on lower level. Continue in this way. Diagram 1 shows position of needle and thread when working stitch on top level; diagram 2 shows a second row of surface honeycomb stitch worked to form a diamond pattern.

Trellis stitch

This consists of two rows of wave stitch (see below), with the second row worked in reverse to form a diamond pattern.

Wave stitch

Work from left to right. Begin with needle to the left of first pleat. Take stitch straight across first and second pleats, with thread below needle. Bring needle out to left of second pleat above stitch just made. Continue in this way until sixth pleat is reached. Have thread above needle for this stitch and bring needle out to left of sixth pleat, just below stitch. Work downward slope to correspond with upward.

FINISHING THE WORK

It should not be necessary to press smocking, but if you feel the embroidery would be improved by a very light pressing, the finished work can be placed face down on an ironing board or thickly-padded table, place a damp cloth over the back of the smocking and pass a warm iron very lightly over it, but do not press flat.

Remove the gathering threads by cutting the knot and back stitch at the side of the work very carefully so as not to damage the fabric, then cut the tied ends (or remove pins) and draw out the gathering threads one by one. Take care not to drag at the gathering thread as it may be caught up in one or two places. The transfer dots may still be noticeable, but usually come out at the first washing.

When you wash the garment, treat it carefully. While the garment is still damp, pull the gathers firmly back into place, and if possible dry flat so the weight of the water does not pull the work out of shape. If necessary, place a damp cloth over the back of the smocking and pass a warm iron lightly over it. Never iron smocking flat.

If smocking becomes stretched with constant wear and washing, it is sometimes possible to restore the shape by whipping the back of the pleats with two or three rows of fine elastic thread.

SOME SAMPLES OF SMOCKING STITCHES

illustrated on pages 84 and 85

All our samples are worked in stranded embroidery cotton, using three strands of cotton. Samples 1–5 each show traditional stitches, suitable for use on any type of garment. Many of these may be combined in the one piece of work.

Sample 6 shows how a variety of stitches may effectively be combined in one piece of work. This is worked on a patterned soft wool fabric, with cream, pink, mauve, light and dark green threads. Stitches, from top to bottom, are as follows: cable stitch in cream; surface honeycomb stitch in pink; outline stitch in cream; cable stitch in light green; bars in dark green – this is simply oversewing two pleats together, by bringing the needle up from the wrong side of the fabric and then stitching over and over the pleats to the required depth; cable stitch in light green; chevron stitch in mauve; outline stitch in cream; two rows of wave stitch, one pink, one mauve; and finally a row of cable stitch in green.

CHILDREN'S DRESSES
Guide to thread quantities

Age	Rows of smocking	Skeins of cotton
1–2 years	11–13	4–5 skeins
3 years	13–15	6 skeins
4 years	17–21	8 skeins
5 years	23–25	9 skeins
6 years	26–27	10 skeins
7–8 years	29–31	12 skeins
9–10 years	31–33	14 skeins

THE PATTERNS

Smocked dress with sleeves

MATERIALS

Of Clark's Anchor Stranded Cotton (USA J. & P. Coats Deluxe Six Strand Floss) — 2 skeins Periwinkle 0119/606, 1 skein White 0402. Pattern for a child's dress suitable for smocking and preferably with a high, round neck and three-quarter length sleeves. Deep rose pink fine wool or other similar fabric — amount quoted in the pattern. A Milward 'Gold Seal' crewel needle No. 6.

STITCHES

Stem; chevron; cable; wave.

DIAGRAMS *(see page 102)*

Diagram A gives a guide to rows of gathers in actual size.

Diagram B shows a section of smocking which is repeated across the fabric. The dotted lines at the left-hand edge indicate the rows of gathers and show the placing of smocking stitches in relation to these rows. The broken vertical lines indicate the folds formed when the gathering threads are drawn up.

TO MAKE

Note. Use 3 strands of cotton throughout.

Cut out dress using paper pattern. Trace the dotted section as given in diagram A on to wrong side of bodice front section. ¾ in. in from top and side edges. Repeat section across width of fabric the number of times required for the dress size you are making, ending ¾ in. from other side.

Following instructions on page 98, gather work on wrong side, using a new thread for each line of dots. Draw up threads, easing gently to form pleats. Do not pull too tightly. Now work smocking stitches following diagram B and stitch and colour key. Do not pull stitches too tightly as the finished work must have elasticity.

TO COMPLETE

Place smocking on an ironing table wrong side up, and cover with a damp cloth. Pass a hot iron lightly over it — do not press. This sets the smocking. Remove all gathering threads and make up dress as instructed in the pattern.

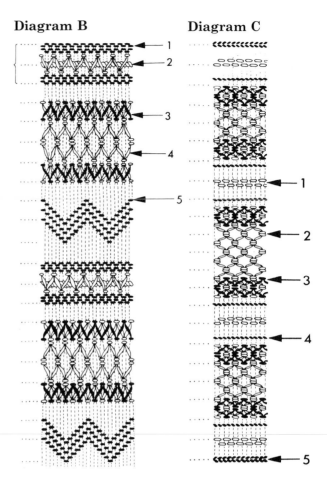

Diagram B

Diagram C

Diagram A

STITCH AND COLOUR KEY (B)
Dress with sleeves

1	Periwinkle	Cable stitch
2	White	Stem stitch
3	Periwinkle	Chevron stitch
4	White	Chevron stitch
5	Periwinkle	Wave stitch

STITCH AND COLOUR KEY (C)
Sleeveless dress

1	Cream	Cable stitch
2	Cream	Chevron stitch
3	Cornflower	Chevron stitch
4	Cornflower	Stem stitch
5	Cornflower	Mock chain stitch

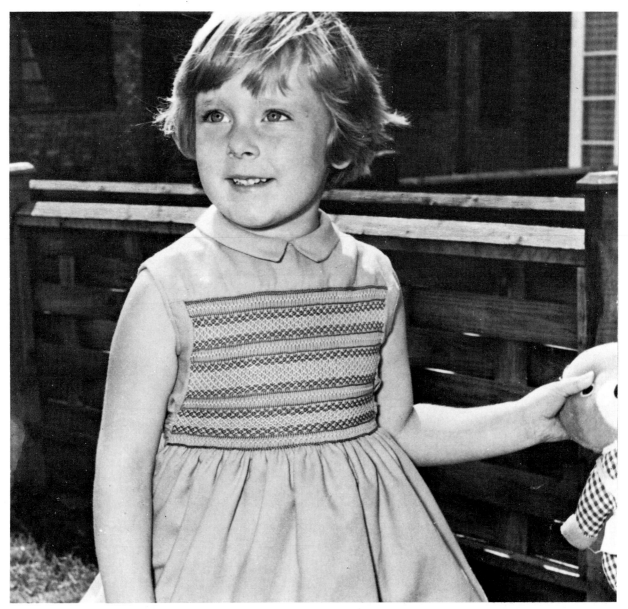

Sleeveless smocked dress

MATERIALS

Of Clark's Anchor Stranded Cotton (USA J. & P. Coats Deluxe Six Strand Floss) — 2 skeins Cream 0386/603, 1 skein Cornflower 0138/594. Pattern for a child's sleeveless dress suitable for smocking. Mid-blue fine wool or other similar fabric — amount quoted in the pattern. A Milward 'Gold Seal' crewel needle No. 6.

STITCHES

Mock chain; chevron; cable; stem.

DIAGRAMS *(see opposite)*

Diagram A gives a guide to rows of gathers in actual size.

Diagram C shows a section of smocking which is repeated across the fabric. The dotted lines at the left-hand edge indicate the rows of gathers and show the placing of smocking stitches in relation to these rows. The broken vertical lines indicate the folds formed when the gathering threads are drawn up.

TO MAKE

Note. Use 4 strands of cotton throughout.

Cut out dress using paper pattern. Trace the dotted section as given in diagram A on to wrong side of bodice front section, ¾ in. in from top and side edges. Repeat section across width of fabric the number of times required for the dress size you are making, ending ¾ in. from other side.

Following instructions on page 98, gather work on wrong side, using a new thread for each line of dots. Draw up threads, easing gently to form pleats. Do not pull too tightly. Now work smocking stitches following diagram B and stitch and colour key. Do not pull stitches too tightly as the finished work must have elasticity.

TO COMPLETE

Place smocking on an ironing table wrong side up, and cover with a damp cloth. Pass a hot iron lightly over it — do not press. This sets the smocking. Remove all gathering threads and make up dress as instructed in the pattern.

Chapter six
PATCHWORK

Mosaic-patterned bag, made from triangular patches of soft leather (see page 111).

There are few needlewomen who do not keep a rag bag – a capacious bag or box into which are tossed all scraps and oddments of fabric left over from dressmaking, embroidery, curtains and cushions – and so on. It is hard indeed to throw away even the tiniest scrap of material in case it will 'come in useful some day'.

The contents of such a rag bag – plus needle and thread – are, in essence, the only raw materials necessary for the beautiful, traditional craft of patchwork. And no special stitches are needed either – just 'plain' sewing.

Patchwork really began as a utilitarian craft, a way of putting fabric oddments to good use, of making do and creating something from nothing. At one time, shapes from scraps of fabric were cut haphazard fashion to any size or form, then an assortment of shapes were joined together to give a flat fabric. Such a disordered method of arrangement, however, was not always pleasing to the eye, and so the geometric approach to patchwork, the devising of definite and symmetrical shapes, evolved. A clever designer today can still use the old method of combining an assortment of shapes and colours and textures, and produce a stunning result – but the approach is not likely to have been a haphazard one, but rather the result of many hours of careful thought and judicious experiment.

A beginner would do better to try out the more conventional geometric patchwork formulae first, and learn how to create pleasing designs with these shapes before moving to freer expressions.

WHAT TO MAKE

Once you have learned to create a fabric from patchwork shapes, you will want to put the fabric to a decorative or practical purpose. A small sampler of your first efforts, perhaps combining different traditional patchwork patterns, can be mounted on a plain backing and used as a pleasing wall decoration.

Many small household items, such as a set of table mats, a needlecase, a tea cosy, or chair back, can be made either from an all-over patchwork fabric or from a plain fabric with patchwork trimming. From these you can progress to more ambitious designs: cushions, curtains, bedcovers, and fashion accessories – an evening stole, for example, or a long party skirt would look spectacular in patchwork.

FABRICS TO USE

Although most types of fabric – with the exception of very sheer and flimsy fabrics – can successfully be used for patchwork, the golden rule to remember is never to mix different weights of fabric in the same design. And if you are likely to want to wash the finished piece, then all the fabrics chosen should have similar washable finishes. Other fabrics which it is best to avoid

are those which stretch out of shape easily, and those which fray.

The best fabrics are the 'stable', crisp ones: cotton is ideal especially as it is available in such a wide range of weights, textures and patterns. Linen is good too; some man-made fibres can be used successfully, but it is best not to combine them with natural fabrics. Velvet can give a wonderfully rich patchwork; wool and wool mixtures also are suitable, and pure silk, although it does need special care in the cutting and sewing, looks luxurious. Leather and suede are good for making patchwork belts, bags and waistcoats, and have the added advantage of not requiring paper shapes – the fabric is sufficiently stiff not to require this extra stabilising.

A Victorian encyclopedia of needlework advises that 'satin, silk and velvet patchwork should be used for cushions, hand-screens, fire-screens, glove and handkerchief cases'. Cloth patchwork on the other hand, it is suggested, should be used for 'carriage rugs, couvrepieds and poor peoples' quilts'. A fine distinction!

TEMPLATES

When patchwork first began to be designed on geometric lines, the shapes which were most used were those which could be easily produced by simple folding of the fabric – e.g. squares, rectangles and diamonds. But when patchwork became more complicated, and the traditional hexagonal shape was devised, it was not so easy to produce regular, even hexagons 'free hand', and so a template was invented: a rigid shape which was used as a pattern over and over again to cut out the fabric patches.

It is possible nowadays to buy plastic or metal templates in a variety of different shapes and sizes, but you can quite easily construct your own from strong, rigid card to suit your particular patchwork requirements. Ideally, for every shape you will have a pair of templates: a solid template, and a window template. The solid template gives the actual size and shape of finished patch; the window template is $\frac{1}{4}$ in. larger on all edges than the solid template, and has the centre area (equal to the solid template) removed. The solid template is used for cutting out the paper linings; the window template is used for cutting the fabric pieces – it can be moved around on the fabric in order to select a pleasing area of pattern. The extra $\frac{1}{4}$ in. on all edges gives a sufficient allowance for turnings.

The best shapes to start with are the hexagon and the diamond, and a pair of templates for each of these shapes is on page 110. These can be traced off and used to make templates, or if you wish a larger or smaller shape then follow these outlines as guides. The diamond shape can be easily adapted to give a triangle shape if required.

To make a hexagon of a specific size you will need a pair of compasses with a pencil. Use the compasses to draw a circle with a radius equal to each side of the hexagon you wish to construct.

Set the compass point anywhere on the circumference of the circle and keeping the same radius on the compasses, mark off a point on the circumference. Now place the compass point at this mark, and mark off another point on the circumference. Continue in this way until six marks have been made on the circumference. Use ruler and pencil to join these points together, and you have your hexagon shape. Cut it out carefully. This gives you a solid template. To make the matching window template, place the solid template on another piece of card and draw carefully round it. Remove solid template, draw another outline outside the first, $\frac{1}{4}$ in. from it all the way round. Cut out on this line, then carefully cut away the centre area.

Other popular traditional shapes: square, rectangle, scale or clamshell, pentagon, octagon, coffin and church window. Different shapes can be used in conjunction with each other to give different design motifs. Octagons used together create areas which have to be filled by squares. Before you start cutting patches from fabric, it is a good idea to cut a variety of paper patches and experiment with these to find an arrangement which pleases you.

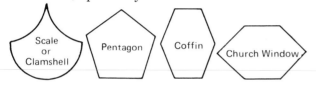

YOU WILL ALSO NEED . . .

Sewing needles and thread to suit the weight of fabrics being used. Pins – good-quality, steel ones are best as they will not mark the fabric. Scissors – two pairs: one for cutting out the fabric shapes, one for cutting the paper linings, both should be well-sharpened and pointed. Paper for making the linings – made do with whatever you can find in the house: old Christmas and birthday cards are ideal as they are fairly stiff. Tailor's chalk, a dressmaker's chalk pencil or an ordinary, well-sharpened lead pencil to mark out patchwork shapes on wrong side of fabric.

CONSTRUCTING A PATCHWORK FABRIC

Although most forms of embroidery depend for their finished effect on neat and careful sewing, with patchwork the primary requisite is accuracy. If each individual patch in a design is not absolutely symmetrical and identical to its neighbour the whole piece will appear 'amateurish' and slipshod. And accuracy begins with cutting the paper lining for each patch absolutely exactly to the right size and shape.

Just as different weights of fabrics should not

be combined in a single piece of work, neither should different weights of paper linings. The papers are used to give crispness and stability to the fabric patches, so sewing is easier. The papers are in fact removed afterwards but even so if different weights and thicknesses of paper are used, this will show in the finished design – some fabric patches may appear a different size to others, puckering may appear in the sewing together, and working with different weights of lined patches will not be particularly easy.

If wished, patches may be lined with non-woven interfacing instead of paper, in which case it is not necessary to remove the linings afterwards.

Using your solid template, place it on the paper you are using for lining, and cut carefully round outside edges of template cutting as close to the edges as possible. Continue in this way to cut the number of paper linings required – linings can be cut from double thickness paper, but never try to cut more than two at once otherwise some are bound to be inaccurate.

When the paper linings are cut, use window template to cut fabric patches. If you are using a patterned fabric, move the template about on the right side of the fabric to find a pleasing area of pattern and then, on the wrong side of fabric, mark out the outline of the template, using chalk, chalk pencil or a lead pencil. Cut out on this line. Continue in this way to cut out the number of fabric patches required.

If you are not using a template (cutting squares or rectangles perhaps) then remember to add $\frac{1}{4}$ in. to all edges for turnings. The next step is to combine the fabric patches with their paper linings. Lay the fabric patch right side down on a clean flat surface, then place paper lining centrally on top of it. Fold down turnings on top of the paper, tucking in corners neatly and pin to hold in place. Now baste turnings in place, being sure to take basting stitches across tucked-in corners; remove pins.

Octagon patches used together create areas which have to be filled with small square patches.

To sew the lined patches together, place the first two patches right sides together, and using a thread to match or contrast with the fabric colour (or if you want to make a special feature of the stitching then use white or black thread) sew the patches together with a fine oversewing or edge-to-edge stitch. Take care not to catch papers in with the stitching. Continue to sew patches together to form design and shape required. If you are making a big or bulky item, then it is usually best to sew patches together in groups, then combine the groups later to avoid having a very heavy piece of work in progress for a long time.

FINISHING TOUCHES

When all your patches are sewn together, carefully remove basting, then press work on the wrong side using an iron setting to suit the fabrics. Now very carefully remove all the paper linings – if these are removed with care they can be kept and used again for another design.

It is usual to line the back of your finished patchwork with a plain-coloured fabric in a weight to suit the fabrics used for the patches. It is also possible to interline a patchwork design, and then work quilting on it to give a superb, quilted patchwork bedcover.

SOME TRADITIONAL PATCHWORK PATTERNS

The easiest design to start with is random patchwork which is, as the name suggests, a random arrangement of different colours and patterns. It is possible however to combine effectively a number of plain and patterned patches so design shapes of groups of patches are created. Or even in a random design by a careful arrangement of strong colours against muted colours the strong colours can be used to form highlights against a background.

After you have cut out your fabric patches, try arranging them on a flat surface, moving them around, and putting them in groups until you find a design arrangement which pleases you. Textures can also be effectively contrasted in patchwork – heavier fabrics such as corduroy and tweeds can be arranged to create an attractive and elegant design.

Hexagon or honeycomb. This is probably the most well-known patchwork pattern, and consists entirely of hexagon patches, arranged either in a random style, or grouped in different colours or patterns. See stole illustrated on page 113.

One traditional arrangement is to surround a dark-coloured patch with six light ones (not necessarily all of same colour or pattern, but light in terms of colour effect). In the angles formed on the outside of the light patches, sew dark patches. Continue in this way.

Diamond. Also a very popular pattern. One effective arrangement is to alternate rows of dark-coloured diamonds with rows of light-coloured diamonds. Alternatively, four similar diamonds can be stitched together to form one very large diamond; continue to arrange patches in groups of four then sew large diamonds together, alternating light and dark.

Mosaic. There are various forms of this traditional pattern. Each is derived from combining different patchwork shapes. One version uses squares and triangles; another uses two different sizes of church windows and squares. By arranging patches carefully in light and dark tones, a fascinating jewel-like pattern is produced.

Jewel. Another pattern using different shapes: squares, rectangles and split squares. To make the split squares (which forms the central 'jewel' part of the design) cut out a large square to size required from card. Now rule a line from the left-hand top corner to the right-hand bottom point. Rule another line horizontally across the centre. Cut down the diagonal line from the left-hand top corner to the centre of the square then cut across to the right on the horizontal line. The two pieces the square is now divided into will be the templates required for the split square. For each split square, combine a dark patch with a light one. Surround each side of the complete square with a rectangle of matching, plain-coloured, medium-toned fabric (to give the effect of a background colour). Fill in the remaining areas with small squares of assorted colours and patterns. The finished effect should give the appearance of large precious stones, set round with smaller ones, in a plain setting. Each of the large squares represents a cut stone with the light falling on it. See long skirt illustrated on page 116.

Canadian or American patchwork. Also known as loghouse quilting, this pattern is traditionally made from several strips of ribbons, arranged to give the appearance of different kinds of wood formed into a succession of squares. The design can be simplified and worked from rectangles of fabric if wished. See table mat illustrated on page 108.

THE PATTERNS

Canadian patchwork table mat

MATERIALS
Small pieces of firm linen or cotton fabric in four
harmonising colours. Piece of lightweight cotton
fabric, 13¼ in. by 19 in. (for foundation). Piece of linen
or cotton fabric, 12¾ in. by 18½ in., in a colour to tone
with patchwork colours (for lining).

MEASUREMENTS
Finished mat measures 12¼ in. by 18 in.

TO MAKE
*Note. This mat is a simplified adaptation of Canadian
or American patchwork, using a similar construction
technique but not an authentic traditional design.*
On the foundation fabric, measure out the centre
widthwise and lengthwise, and mark across the fabric

with basting stitches.
From the firm linen or cotton fabric pieces, cut out
individual shapes as follows:

1 7½ in. by 2¾ in.
2 2¾ in. by 4½ in.
3 9¼ in. by 4½ in.
4 4½ in. by 4½ in.
5 11 in. by 4½ in.
6 8 in. by 4½ in.
7 12¾ in. by 4½ in.
8 8 in. by 4½ in.
9 12¾ in. by 4½ in.
10 13¼ in. by 5½ in.
11 16¾ in. by 4½ in.
12 11½ in. by 5¼ in.
13 14½ in. by 4½ in.

With one long side of foundation fabric towards you,
baste patch No. 1 on to foundation fabric, positioning it
centrally on crossed basting stitches, and having the
strip running horizontally across fabric. All other
patches are folded in half lengthwise, wrong sides
together, before stitching in place to form the patchwork
pattern. Work clockwise, from the centre outwards, and

108

placing each patch in numerical order. Have all folds facing towards the centre and where edges overlap, allow ½ in. for the overlap.

For instance, patch No. 2 should first be folded and pressed along its fold, then placed at right-hand edge of patch No. 1, so fold of No. 2 overlaps right-hand edge of No. 1 by ½ in. Stitch No. 2 to No. 1 with neat slipstitches along folded edge.

Now place folded and pressed patch No. 3 so its folded edge overlaps bottom edges of Nos. 1 and 2 by ½ in. Slipstitch in place along folded edge, as before.

Continue placing and stitching patches in this way, following diagram, right, as a guide to positions and overlaps of each patch.

TO COMPLETE

Fold back ½ in. on all outside edges of finished patchwork to wrong side. Baste, then press well. Turn in ¼ in. on all edges of lining fabric, and press. Place lining against patchwork, wrong sides facing, and slipstitch neatly together round all edges. Press.

Long skirt with jewel patchwork border
illustrated in colour on page 116

MATERIALS

2½ yd. soft wool fabric, 36 in. wide, in black (or colour preferred). Scraps of plain and patterned fabric for patchwork. Paper for linings. 1 yd. petersham ribbon, 1½ in. wide. A 7-in. zip fastener. Two press fasteners and two hooks and eyes.

MEASUREMENTS

As skirt is gathered on to waistband, it can be made to fit any waist size (see instructions below). Depth of patchwork border: 5 in.

TO MAKE

Cut two pieces of fabric, each 36 in. by 43 in. Cut a 4-in. wide strip of fabric to the size of your waist plus 3 in. Cut petersham ribbon to this same length.

Place two main fabric sections together, right sides facing, and with ½-in. turnings, stitch long edges together to form side seams of skirt. Leave left side seam open for 7 in. from waist edge for zip opening.

Run two rows of gathering stitches round waist edge of

ARRANGEMENT OF THE PATCHES

skirt, and insert zip into left side opening. To make waistband, fold long strip of fabric in half lengthwise, slip petersham ribbon inside folded strip so edge of ribbon is against inside of fold. Baste in place. The folded edge will be the top of the waistband. On one side smooth fabric down and under bottom edge of petersham, and baste in place. This will be the right side of waistband. Now draw up gathers on skirt to fit waist size plus 1 in. for ease. Place gathered edge under right-side edge of waistband, adjusting gathers to fit, and having 2-in. overlap on waistband extending from back waistband. Baste in place. Turn under remaining edge on inside edge of waistband, and covering all raw edges, baste in place. Stitch along bottom edge of waistband, through all fabric thicknesses and stitching from right side of skirt. Turn up lower hem to length required, and stitch neatly. Fasten waist overlap with hooks and eyes and press fasteners.

To work patchwork border

The diagrams below give the four template shapes you need, in actual size. Using these as a guide make your own templates from stiff card, making matching

TEMPLATES (actual size)

(NOTE: CUT FABRIC ¼ in. WIDER ALL ROUND TEMPLATE)

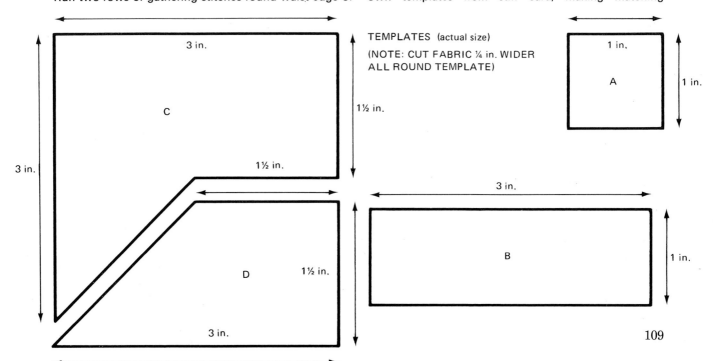

window templates, if wished, for each shape.
Using these templates, cut out the shapes as follows: shape A – 56 each in fabric and paper; shape B – 56 each in fabric and paper; shape C – 14 each in fabric and paper; shape D – 14 each in fabric and paper. If you have not made window templates, then remember to add $\frac{1}{4}$ in. to all edges when cutting out fabric patches. Alternate fabric colours and patterns as much as possible for each shape.

Following diagram, right, arrange four A shapes, four B shapes, one C and one D to form the complete jewel patchwork square. Be sure the colour and pattern of each shape forms a good contrast against the adjacent shape. Stitch shapes together.

Make thirteen more similar jewel patchwork squares, then sew all the squares together to form one long strip.

TO COMPLETE
Stitch border to skirt, $\frac{3}{4}$ in. up from lower edge.

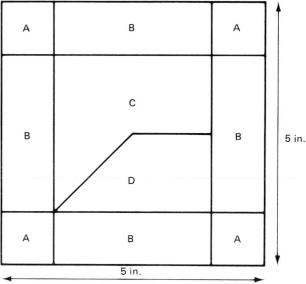

Arrangement of shapes to form square patch

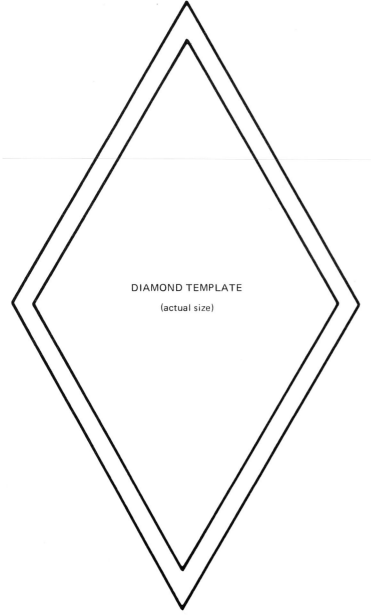

DIAMOND TEMPLATE

(actual size)

Gardening apron
illustrated on pages 117 and 120

MATERIALS
1 yd. cotton fabric, 36 in. wide, in green (or colour preferred). Scraps of patterned cotton fabric for patchwork. Paper for linings. $1\frac{1}{2}$ yd. cotton tape, 1 in. wide.

MEASUREMENTS
Finished apron (excluding tapes) measures 32 in. long and 24 in. wide (at widest point).

TO MAKE YOUR PATTERN
The diagram opposite gives the pattern you will need for the apron: 1 square on the diagram equals 1 inch. Mark out a large sheet of strong brown or white paper into 1-in. squares, then copy the pattern piece as given in the miniature diagram on to your full-size grid. Each of the squares on the miniature diagram represents one square on your paper. Copy the outlines and positions of lines, curves and angles in relation to the squares as accurately as possible. Cut out the pattern piece.

TO MAKE
Using your paper pattern, cut out the apron main piece from double thickness fabric, placing centre front edge of pattern on fabric fold as indicated. Turn in and

HEXAGON TEMPLATE

(actual size)

stitch ½-in. hems on all raw edges of apron, and a 1-in. hem at lower edge.

Make patchwork

On the opposite page are the templates for diamond and hexagon shapes in actual size. Following the inner lines as a guide for the actual size template, and the outer lines as a guide for the window templates, construct your own templates from stiff card.

Using these templates, cut out ten diamond shapes (six will be used for flower petals, four for leaves) and one hexagon for flower centre. Use actual size template for cutting paper linings; window templates for fabric. Cut a strip of patterned cotton 16 in. long and 1½ in. wide for the flower stalk. Turn in and stitch a ¾-in. hem on all edges.

TO COMPLETE

Arrange shapes on apron to form flower. Baste and stitch in position. Press.

Mosaic-patterned bag

illustrated on page 104

MATERIALS

Assorted offcuts of suede or soft leather (these can usually be bought cheaply in bags or by weight from leather craft shops or warehouses). Two strips of soft black leather, each 14 in. by 3½ in. (for finishing top edge of bag). One strip of black leather, 60 in. by 1¼ in., for handle (a dog leash could be used instead). ½ yd. cotton fabric, 36 in. wide, for lining. Two 1½-in. split rings, and two dog leash clips. Fabric glue. Suitable needle and thread for sewing leather (strong waxed linen thread is ideal).

MEASUREMENTS

Finished size of bag (excluding handles) is 13 in. by 16½ in.

TO MAKE

The diagram below gives the template for the triangular mosaic shape in actual size. Using this as a guide make your own template from stiff card. As leather has considerably more stability than fabric, there is no need to cut paper linings for this patchwork, so only this one template will be required. Using it as a guide, cut out forty-two shapes in leather.

Arrange three rows of thirteen shapes each into mosaic patchwork pattern. Square off ends of row with half triangles cut from the remaining shapes.

Having the row of shapes arranged horizontally in

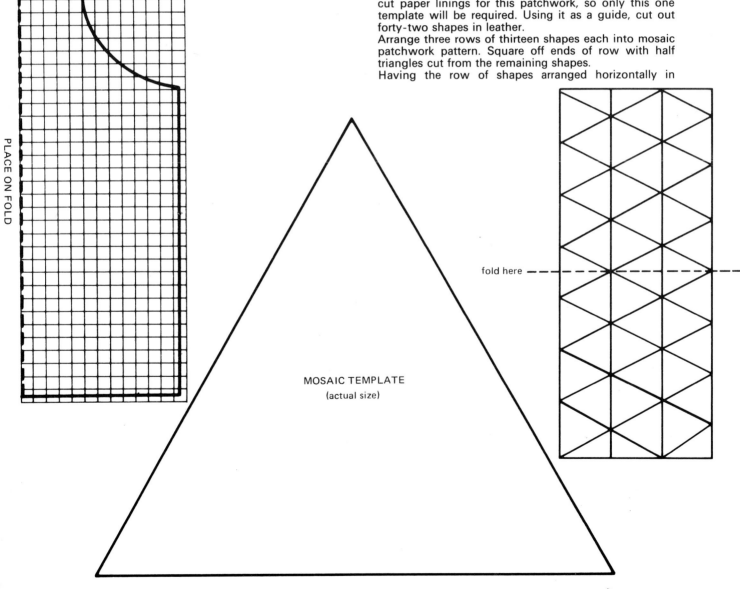

PLACE ON FOLD

1 square = 1 inch

MOSAIC TEMPLATE
(actual size)

fold here

5½ in.

front of you, and working from left to right, stitch each row of shapes together by overlapping right-hand edge of first shape $\frac{1}{4}$ in. over left-hand edge of shape next to it. This will be made easier if you draw a light pencil guideline on the underlapping leather shape first.

When each of the three rows is firmly stitched together, join the three rows together (see diagram on previous page for finished arrangement). Stitch long seams with $\frac{1}{4}$-in. turnings, right sides of rows together. Press seams open.

Stitch one strip of soft black leather to each short end of patchwork, right sides together, and taking $\frac{1}{4}$-in. turnings. Fold patchwork in half across the length (see diagram on previous page) right sides together, stitch side seams. Take $\frac{1}{4}$-in. turnings, and open out black strips at either end to give a long continuous seam. Turn bag right side out, and fold black leather strips inside top of bag, leaving an edging of $\frac{5}{8}$ in. showing on right side of bag. Stick leather lightly down on inside with fabric glue.

Make up cotton lining to fit bag and insert into bag, wrong sides together. Turn in top edges of lining to 2 in. below bag opening, and neatly slipstitch to black leather to hold lining in place.

Punch a hole through both sides of bag, 1 in. from each side seam and insert a metal split ring through each set of holes. To make handle, mark centre line on wrong side of leather strip along its length. Fold outside edge to meet this line and stick lightly in place with fabric glue. Stitch along each edge. Loop each end of handle through a dog leash clip and stitch firmly. Fasten clips to rings at either side of bag to make a long handle. To make a shorter handle, loop handle through one ring on bag, and fasten both clips to ring at other side.

Stole with honeycomb patchwork

MATERIALS
2 yd. fabric, 36 in. wide, for the stole, and $\frac{1}{4}$ yd. in each of four contrasting colours, 36 in. wide, for the patchwork (or use scraps from the rag bag). Paper for linings.

MEASUREMENTS
Finished stole measures $17\frac{1}{2}$ in. wide and just under 2 yd. long.

TO MAKE
Cut stole fabric into two equal pieces, each 18 in. by 2 yd.: one piece will form right side of stole, the other will form the lining.

Make patchwork
The diagram below gives the hexagonal template in actual size. Following the inner line as a guide for the actual size template, and the outer line as a guide for the window template, construct your own pair of hexagonal templates from stiff card.

Make honeycomb motifs first: you will need a total of 56 hexagons altogether – use window template to cut out fabric hexagons, actual size template to cut out paper linings. Each motif is formed by sewing six matching hexagons round a central hexagon in a contrast colour. Make eight motifs altogether, two in each colour, contrasting the colour of the central hexagon in each motif.

To make each honeycomb border, cut eight hexagons in one colour, and eight in a contrasting colour. Join one set of hexagons (all the same colour) into a row, then join the second set, arranging the hexagons in this set so there are seven whole hexagons and one half hexagon at each end of the row. Join the two rows together to form honeycomb pattern. Make second border in a similar way.

To assemble stole
From one of the patchwork colours not used in the honeycomb borders, cut two strips, each 18 in. long and $1\frac{1}{4}$ in. wide. Turn in and baste $\frac{1}{4}$ in. along one long side of each strip. Baste strips to right side of stole, positioning a strip $1\frac{3}{4}$ in. from each short end of stole, and having the turned-in edge of strip to the outside. (i.e. pointing towards short end of stole). Carefully slipstitch strips to stole along turned-in edges.

Now sew a honeycomb border to each end of stole, arranging the hexagons to overlap the contrast strip, with the points of the hexagons just touching the turned-in edge of the contrast strip (see diagram below). If necessary, trim width of stole to correspond with honeycomb borders. Arrange honeycomb motifs at regular intervals along length of stole, between honeycomb borders. Baste in position, then sew carefully in place, using slipstitches and translucent thread.

TO COMPLETE
Place right side of stole against lining, right sides facing, and stitch round all sides $\frac{1}{4}$ in. from edges of fabric, and leaving 10 in. open in the centre of one long seam. Turn stole right side out through this opening, turn in remaining raw edges and slipstitch neatly together. Press stole carefully on the wrong side.

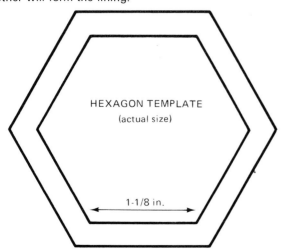

HEXAGON TEMPLATE
(actual size)

1-1/8 in.

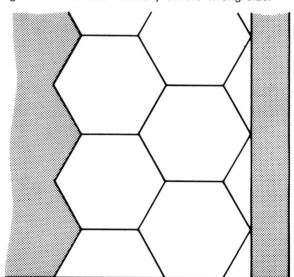

CORNER OF STOLE SHOWING ARRANGEMENT OF HONEYCOMB BORDER AGAINST CONTRAST STRIP

Party stole has honeycomb patchwork borders and motifs.

Chapter seven
APPLIQUÉ

'Willow stump', an impressive modern embroidery in which raffia, beads, gold threads and gold kid are applied to a green silk ground. Decorative surface stitchery is in wools, silks and cottons.

Of all forms of decorative needlework, appliqué probably gives the greatest scope for original design. For this reason, beginners often shy away from the craft, preferring to work one of the more 'regimented' forms of embroidery where expression is of necessity controlled by a formalised stitching technique. And yet appliqué can be extremely simple, easy to work and still wonderfully effective.

Briefly, appliqué is created by 'applying' – hence, 'appliqué' – several fabrics to a background fabric. The applied fabrics are cut into decorative shapes and stitched in place to form a pleasing arrangement of colour and shape on the background fabric. Further interest can be added to the design with embroidery stitching used either to hold the fabric shapes in place, or merely as a surface decoration.

Any piece of needlework in which one fabric is applied to another, even if it is only a single flower motif stitched to the centre of a handkerchief, can be termed appliqué. Designs can take the form of simple decorations on fashion accessories or household linen and soft furnishings right through to the most elaborate picture or wall hanging. The design itself can be representative, pictorial or purely abstract. In abstract designs, the imagination of the worker is given full scope for expression!

Many people are confused by the difference between appliqué and collage. In simple terms, in appliqué the fabrics are held in place by stitching, plain or decorative; in collage the applied pieces – which can be fabrics, or any other materials from bent nails through to feathers and plastic buttons – are secured by glueing. Appliqué therefore is a needlecraft; collage simply a fascinating handicraft.

FABRICS

As with patchwork, your rag bag is invaluable as a starting-off point for an appliqué design. Have a look through your store of fabric oddments, and you'll be surprised how many can spark off an idea. A pretty print, for example, can have one repeat of the pattern cut out and used as a motif to brighten the corner of a plain table mat. Or you may find several fabrics which tone nicely together – cut out shapes from these fabrics and try arranging them in different groupings against a plain piece of fabric . . . In no time at all you will have constructed your first appliqué picture!

Most fabrics are suitable for background materials, depending on the sort of design you intend to create, and whether the background fabric is to be an important part of the design. If, for instance, the background is merely to give a base on which to stitch your applied fabrics, and little if any of the background will be visible in the finished design, then any smooth, stable fabric such as calico or a firm linen is suitable.

On the other hand, if the background fabric is to feature in your design then a fabric should be chosen with particular characteristics depending on whether you want a smooth, muted background, or one with an interesting texture, or a strong colour (because your applied shapes will be in muted or toning shades), or a pattern (to contrast with plain applied shapes). Whichever fabric you choose however, ideally it should not be too thick, it should be relatively stable, and it should not be too easily stretched or pulled out of shape.

The applied fabrics again can be of many types but, as with the background fabric, they should not stretch or pucker easily, or be too bulky. Fabrics which do not fray easily are the easiest to work with – felt, plastic and leather are excellent as they are all fray-free fabrics. Other fabrics can have their edges treated in various ways (see page 118) to prevent fraying. In blind appliqué, the edges of all applied fabrics are turned under before the shapes are stitched to the background, so as non-fraying qualities are then not so important the choice of suitable fabrics is much wider.

Cotton on cotton appliqués, and linen on linen give good hardwearing results, ideal for household furnishings and clothes. For luxury appliqués, velvets, brocades, silks, laces and satins give wonderfully rich results but of course are not recommended for everyday items which have to withstand constant wear and tear! Applied fabrics do not have to be similar to the background, or even to each other, but if you are likely to want to wash the finished design, then all the fabrics used including background should have similar washable qualities.

It is preferable, especially for your first efforts at appliqué, to choose fabrics of similar weights – if you try to combine a fairly thick fabric with some thin ones, you will probably end up with a puckered, badly-applied design.

THREADS

Thread can be synthetic, cotton, wool or silk depending on the fabrics being used in the design. The colour will depend on whether the stitching is to form a focal point of the design. If it is not, and therefore should be as invisible as possible, then use thread in a colour either to match the background fabric, or else use a different thread colour for each applied shape, to match the individual fabrics.

Alternatively, if stitching is to be part of the design, then use thread colours to tone or contrast with the fabrics. Sometimes the fabrics are stitched in place with matching threads, and then decorative surface stitching worked over the design in toning or contrasting embroidery threads.

YOU WILL ALSO NEED . . .

Needles to suit threads being used; good-quality rustless pins; basting thread; paper and pencil for trying out design ideas; scissors – one sharp pair for cutting out your fabric shapes, another for cutting threads; dressmaker's tracing paper, pounce, chalk, or watercolour paint and brush depending on which method you choose for transferring your designs to your background fabrics; iron-on interfacing (useful for giving extra 'body' to flimsy fabrics, and so prevent puckering); fabric glue (to treat edges of sheer fabrics); an embroidery frame, if you are working on an appliqué picture, or other large design, where it is imperative that the background fabric is kept taut.

WORKING METHODS

The first step in any appliqué is to plan your design. This is as important for a simple piece of work using only a single applied motif, as it is for a complex abstract picture. Try sketching out a rough idea of your design on a piece of paper first of all, so you can get some idea of the size and shape of the pieces you want, and their

'Feather' appliqué sample. Black organza applied to ground fabric and held in place with stitchery.

Above: *close-up of honeycomb patchwork border on evening stole (see page 112).* **Above right:** *patchwork flower on gardening apron (see page 110).* **Right:** *blind appliqué motifs on smock (see page 121).*

Opposite: *elegant long skirt with jewel patchwork hem border (see page 109).*

Towelling motifs applied to a cotton ground.

grouping and positions on the background. When you think you have established the sort of shapes you want to use – or even if you are still undecided – try cutting out shapes from paper and moving these about on your background fabric until you find a pleasing arrangement.

The next step is to transfer the design to your background. Again, even if it is only a simple design with one or two applied pieces, an accurate indication on your background of positions of the applied shapes will make working much easier. Designs can be transferred by any of the methods described on page 8. Alternatively, if you have used paper shapes to arrive at your design, then these may be pinned in place, and drawn round with watercolour paint, or with basting stitches.

If you are working on a picture, or large design, then mount background fabric on a frame – follow instructions for framing-up canvas on page 66, substituting the background fabric of your choice for the canvas. Small designs can be worked on a circular embroidery frame (see page 8).

PREPARING FABRICS

When you have established the shapes you want to use, cut them out from your fabrics – if you have used paper shapes as an initial guide, these again will come in useful for they can be used as paper patterns for cutting out fabrics. If you intend to turn in raw edges of the fabric shapes, then remember to add on an allowance for turnings to all edges – $\frac{1}{4}$ in. should be sufficient for most fabrics.

Another important point to remember when cutting out fabrics is that, if possible, the grain should run in the same direction when pieces are applied; the grain of the background fabric should also run in the same direction to avoid puckering. Ideally the grain should run downwards through all the fabrics but this may not always be possible. It is best in any case not to let yourself be too restricted by a slavish addiction to the grain-rule – otherwise the spontaneity of your design may suffer!

If the fabric is liable to fray and you are not turning in the edges, then it is advisable to oversew lightly round the edges of each shape. Alternatively, iron-on interfacing can be applied to the backs of the shapes, to give them extra stability; or a light coating of a fabric adhesive can be painted round the edges of the fabric, on the wrong side, and allowed to dry.

If you are working blind appliqué, run a line of machine stitching round your shape along the line where the turning is to be. This will give a clean, neat edge for turning. Clip into turnings carefully, especially on curved edges, then fold turnings to wrong side. Pin or baste to hold in place. Press if necessary.

ASSEMBLING YOUR DESIGN

Now arrange your prepared fabric shapes on your backing fabric, pin in place, then baste. If you have overlapping pieces, you can, if you wish, trim away the excess fabric from the underneath fabric, so the work does not become too bulky. Nets and similar fine transparent fabrics can be used to great effect either by partially overlapping other fabrics, or by laying a complete piece of transparent fabric over the entire appliqué when other pieces are stitched in position.

When pinning pieces in place insert pins horizontally across work. When basting, take stitches slanting downwards in lines right across work. If you try to baste round each fabric shape, this tends to distort the piece and cause a 'bubble' to form in the centre. The best order to follow is to pin and subsequently baste the pieces which go at the back of the work first and work towards the front.

When basting is complete begin to stitch your fabric shapes to the background fabric. The type of stitching you use will depend on the design you are working, whether it needs to be securely fastened to withstand hard wear, and whether or not stitching is to form a decorative part of the finished design.

A straightforward stitching method is merely to take tiny, straight stitches through fabric and backing, always bringing needle up through the backing fabric, and taking it down into the applied fabric. For blind appliqué, stitch pieces in place with tiny slip stitches which will be virtually invisible in the finished design.

If the design will not have to withstand a lot of wear and tear, then various types of decorative stitching can be used to secure the applied shapes. For instance, a long piece of applied fabric (perhaps a length of lace or similar ornamental braid) could simply be secured by single stitches taken right across the width of the applied piece at regular intervals, using a thread to contrast or tone with the appliqué fabric. A circular motif could have small blanket or

Silk, cotton and suede shapes applied to silk, with some shapes padded with foam rubber.

buttonhole stitches worked over its edge at evenly-spaced intervals.

When applied shapes are all stitched to the background fabric, further interest can if wished be added to the design by working decorative surface embroidery stitching. In one very old traditional appliqué technique, couched threads are worked round the edges of all applied pieces.

Other embroidery techniques and stitches which can be effectively used on appliqué designs are: padded satin stitch, split stitches, stem stitch, chain and detached chain stitches, French knots, cretan stitch, back stitches – and many more (see chapter one for working instructions for these stitches). You will soon learn to recognise how a particular embroidery stitch can add interest to an appliqué design, and complement the fabric shapes and colours you have used. Beads, buttons, sequins and other small trimmings can also effectively be used.

Sometimes a design which appears somewhat weak when all the fabric shapes are stitched in place can be strengthened with the judicious use of surface stitching. On the other hand it is important to guard against overdoing a design . . . add too much, and you will end by overstating rather than understating a design idea.

If you have used a frame for your work, normally the only finishing necessary after removing basting stitches will be a light press on the wrong side. If there is slight puckering, then steam pressing should flatten out the piece. However, if the fabric is badly stretched out of true or puckered, then the whole piece will have to be thoroughly stretched. Follow instructions on page 73 for stretching canvas embroideries.

APPLIQUÉ TECHNIQUES

Inlaid appliqué. In this technique the design is worked out with great precision, then the shapes where fabrics are to be applied are cut away from the background material, and the applied fabrics carefully fitted into these holes. There is no overlap, and usually the point where the edges meet is covered with a couched thread or cord.

Whitework appliqué. As the name implies, white fabric shapes are applied to a white background fabric.

Decoupé appliqué. The principle in this work is similar to inlaid appliqué, with buttonhole or blanket stitches worked over the cut edges instead of couching.

San Blas appliqué. This technique which comes from the San Blas Islands, off Panama, is really a sort of appliqué in reverse for, instead of building up layers of fabrics, the design is created by cutting away areas of fabric. Usually worked in brightly-coloured plain cotton, the design starts with up to five or six layers of cotton placed together, and basted round the edges. Areas are then cut away to reveal the required colour beneath. Often the bottom layer of cloth is black, and in order to reach this ground colour it will be necessary in parts to cut through five layers of top fabrics.

Broderie suisse appliqué. In this, white cambric or muslin is used for the applied fabric, coloured satin or silk for the background. The muslin or cambric is first embroidered with chain stitch in a suitable pattern, and then shapes cut out and stitched in place to the background with open buttonhole or feather stitching.

119

Gardening apron, with patchwork flower motif (see page 110).

THE PATTERNS

Blind appliqué border for a smock

MATERIALS

A suitable smock with yoke, in a natural calico or firm cotton fabric. Scraps of coloured cotton fabric (we used five different colours for our appliqué – bright pink, medium purple, dark purple, yellow and a pink and blue check). Transparent nylon sewing thread.

TO MAKE

The diagrams on page 122 give the templates you need in actual size. Using these as a guide, construct your own templates from stiff card. Using these templates, cut out fabric shapes as follows: 12 of shape A (bright pink); 12 of shape B (dark purple); 12 of shape C (checked fabric); 5 of shape D (yellow); 13 of shape E (medium purple). Turn in and baste ¼ in. round the edge of each shape. Press shapes flat.

There are two basic motifs in the border design: the

Star Motif formed from two A shapes and two B shapes; the Cross Motif formed from two C shapes, one D and one E. To arrange each Star Motif, first place the two B shapes to form an 'X' then place the two A shapes on top of the 'X' to form an upright cross, with its centre overlapping the centre of the 'X'.

To arrange each Cross Motif, first place the two C shapes to form an upright cross, then place the D shape exactly on centre of the cross, and then finally place the E shape exactly on the centre of the D shape.

Pin then baste a cross motif to the centre front of smock yoke, with a star motif on either side of the centre cross motif. Using nylon thread, and following method given on page 118 for stitching blind appliqué, stitch each motif to the smock.

Space the remaining four star motifs and four cross motifs evenly round hem of smock in an alternate pattern of crosses and stars. Baste then stitch in place. Stitch remaining E motifs between each cross and star motif round the hem of smock.

(Note. It may be necessary to have more or fewer motifs round hem of smock, depending on the width of the smock.)

CROSS MOTIF templates (actual size)

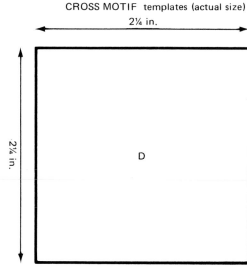

2¼ in.

2¼ in.

D

4 in.

1 in.

A

1¼ in.

1¼ in.

E

4 in.

1-1/8 in.

B

STAR MOTIF templates (actual size)

1¾ in.

4¼ in.

C

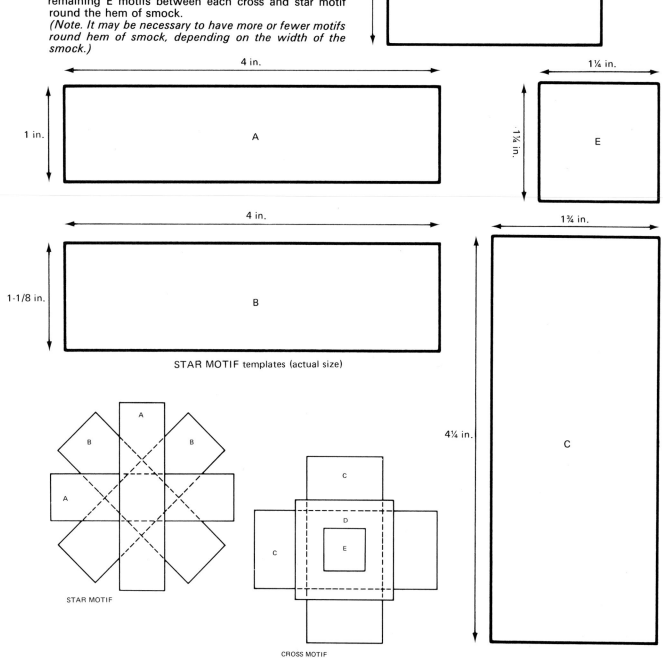

STAR MOTIF

CROSS MOTIF

122

Appliqué bolero with surface stitchery

MATERIALS
1¾ yd. denim or canvas fabric, 36 in. wide. Oddments of cotton fabric for appliqué in three colours (plain or patterned). 4 yd. ric-rac braid. Stranded embroidery cotton to contrast or tone with appliqué fabrics.

MEASUREMENTS
The bolero is fairly loose-fitting so should comfortably fit chest size 28–30 in.; length at centre back 18¾ in.

TO MAKE YOUR PATTERN
The diagram on page 126 gives the pattern you will need for the bolero: one square on the diagram equals 1 in. Mark out a large sheet of strong brown or white paper into 1-in. squares, then copy the pattern pieces as given in the miniature diagram on to your full-size grid. Each of the squares on the miniature diagram represents

continued on page 126

Opposite: *reversible quilted jacket with feather pattern (see page 138).*

Right: *hessian (burlap) cushion cover with drawn-thread embroidery. The Florentine pattern is worked in crewel wool, in yellow and three shades of red, worked in the 4:2 step, with a variable number of stitches to each step.*

Below: *Italian quilted evening bag (see page 141).*

one square on your paper. Copy the outlines and positions of lines, curves and angles in relation to the squares as accurately as possible. Cut out the two pattern pieces.

TO MAKE

Using your paper pattern, cut out bolero back and front pieces twice from folded fabric. This gives one set of pieces for right side of bolero; one set for the lining. Be sure to place centre back of back section to fold of fabric, as indicated on the pattern diagram. Working with pieces for right side of bolero, stitch fronts to back along shoulders and side seams, right sides together, and taking ½-in. turnings. Press seams open.

The diagrams opposite give the templates you need for the appliqué shapes in actual size. Using these as a guide, construct your own templates from stiff card.

Using your templates, cut out four of shape A in first fabric, two of shape B in second fabric, and two of shape C in third fabric. Turn in raw edges round each shape and baste. Place, baste and oversew shapes in position to right side of bolero, arranging the shapes as shown in photograph on page 123 (or in any arrangement wished).

TO WORK EMBROIDERY

Shapes B and C are outlined with one row of stem stitch. Shapes A have a double cross stitch in the centre, seven French knots spaced evenly round the star, one row of chain stitch and one row of stem stitch round outside of shape. Two shapes A (at right and left centre fronts) have sixteen detached chain stitches spaced evenly round the outer circle of stem stitch.

TO COMPLETE

Turn in and baste ½ in. round armholes, neck, front opening and lower edge of bolero. Stitch ric-rac braid round all these edges, ¼ in. from folded edge of garment.

Sew shoulder and side seams of lining back and fronts, right sides together and taking ½-in. turnings. Press seams open. Place lining inside bolero, wrong sides together. Turn in raw edges of lining round all outer edges and slipstitch neatly to inside of bolero.

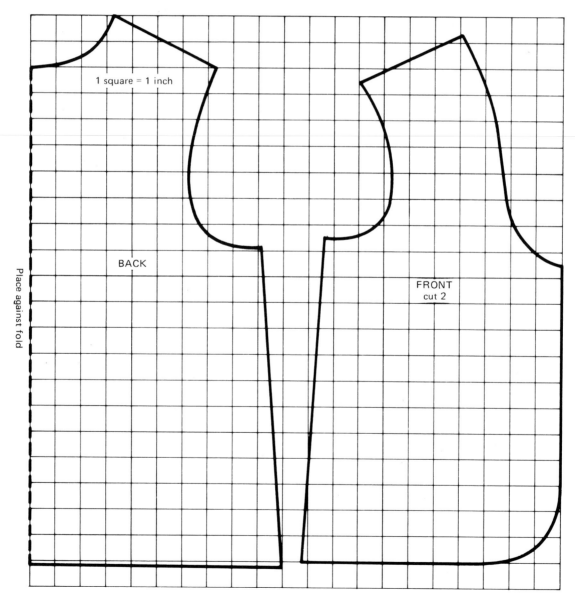

1 square = 1 inch

Place against fold

BACK

FRONT
cut 2

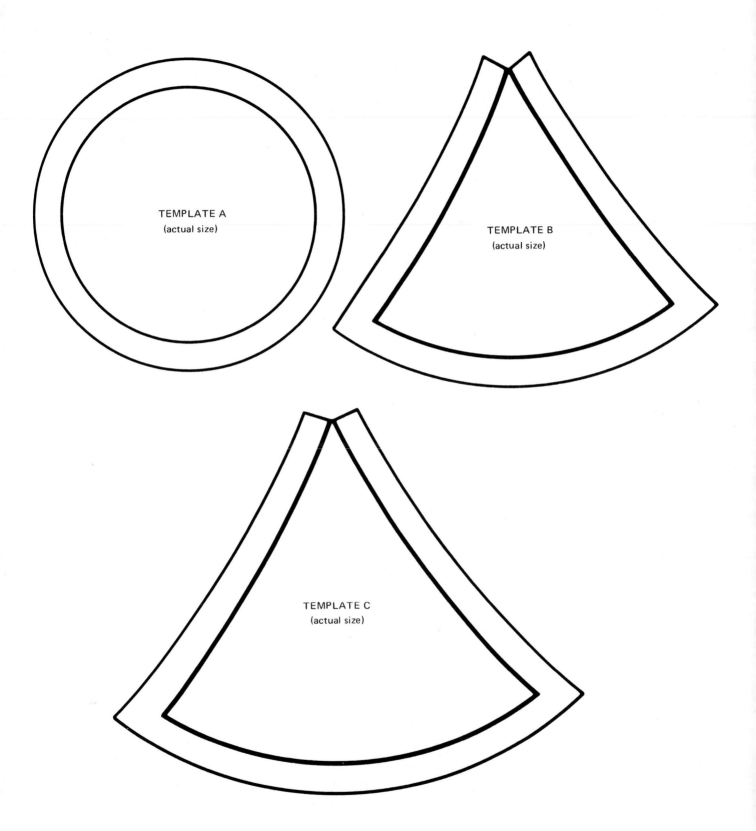

TEMPLATE A
(actual size)

TEMPLATE B
(actual size)

TEMPLATE C
(actual size)

Beach bag and sun glasses case

MATERIALS

For bag : two pieces of blue felt, each 25 in. by 18 in.; $\frac{1}{4}$ yd. white felt, 27 in. wide; one 9-in. square of yellow felt; small squares or scraps of yellow, orange, scarlet and black felt. Two round plastic bag handles in black with a $5\frac{1}{2}$-in. diameter.

For sun glasses case : one 9-in. square each in blue and orange felt, plus small squares or scraps of orange and black felt.

MEASUREMENTS

Finished bag measures approximately 24 in. wide by 20 in. deep (including handles). Sun glasses case measures $4\frac{1}{2}$ in. by 9 in.

TO MAKE
Beach bag

The diagrams opposite, on squared paper, give the pattern pieces you will need for the two cloud shapes: 1 square on the diagram equals 1 in. Mark out a sheet of strong brown or white paper into 1-in. squares, then copy the pattern pieces as given in the miniature diagrams on to your full-size grid. Each of the squares

on the miniature diagrams represents one square on your paper. Copy the outlines and positions of lines, curves and angles in relation to the squares as accurately as possible. Cut out the pattern pieces.

The diagrams on page 130 show the pattern pieces you need in actual size: sun, two sunray shapes, mouth, nose, eye, and eyebrow. Using these as a guide, make your own paper pattern for these shapes.

Now using your paper pattern pieces, cut out one each of the two cloud shapes from white felt, the sun from yellow felt, and remaining pieces as indicated on pattern diagrams. Lay one piece of blue felt on a flat surface, so shorter ends are at the sides. Pin yellow sun to blue felt, positioning it 3 in. up from lower edge, and midway between side edges. Pin clouds in position, fitting them on to sun as indicated on pattern diagram. Stitch sun and clouds in position, using matching thread for each piece. Now pin sunray pieces in position round sun, alternating colours (if wished, the bigger sunray pieces may slightly overlap the smaller sunrays). Stitch these in place. Finally pin then stitch face pieces in position, following pattern diagrams. Place appliquéd felt and plain felt piece together, right sides facing, and stitch side and lower edge seams with $\frac{1}{2}$-in. turnings. Leave side seams unstitched for $6\frac{1}{2}$ in. at top of bag. Turn in and stitch $\frac{1}{2}$-in. hems along these edges. Turn in and stitch a 1-in. channel along top edge of each side of bag. Turn bag right side out and thread a plastic handle through channel on each side.

Sun glasses case

Cut the squares of blue and orange felt in half, to give four oblong strips, each $4\frac{1}{2}$ in. by 9 in. The diagrams below give the pattern pieces you will need in actual size. Using these as a guide, make your own paper pattern for the main shape, and the inner circle shape. Using your paper pattern, cut out the main shape once from orange felt, the inner circle shape twice from black felt. Place a black circle centrally on each orange circle of main piece and stitch in place using black thread and stitching near edge of black circle. Now place appliqué motif centrally on one oblong of blue felt. Stitch in place with orange thread, round edges of shape. Place the four felt oblongs together, so the blue piece with appliqué is uppermost, the plain blue piece is underneath, and the two orange pieces are sandwiched between. Machine stitch down both long sides and across one short end, taking a $\frac{1}{4}$-in. seam.

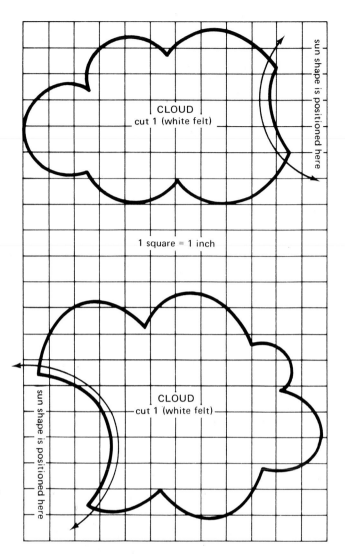

CLOUD
cut 1 (white felt)

sun shape is positioned here

1 square = 1 inch

CLOUD
cut 1 (white felt)

sun shape is positioned here

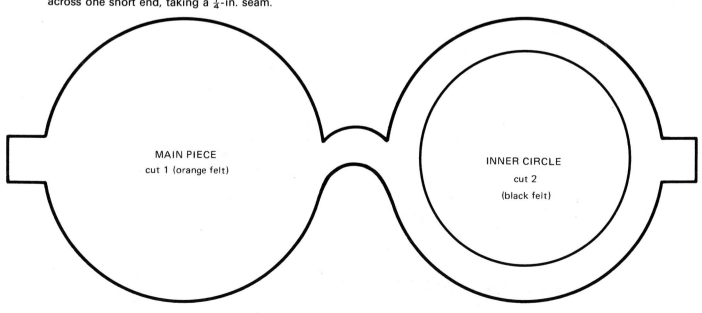

MAIN PIECE
cut 1 (orange felt)

INNER CIRCLE
cut 2
(black felt)

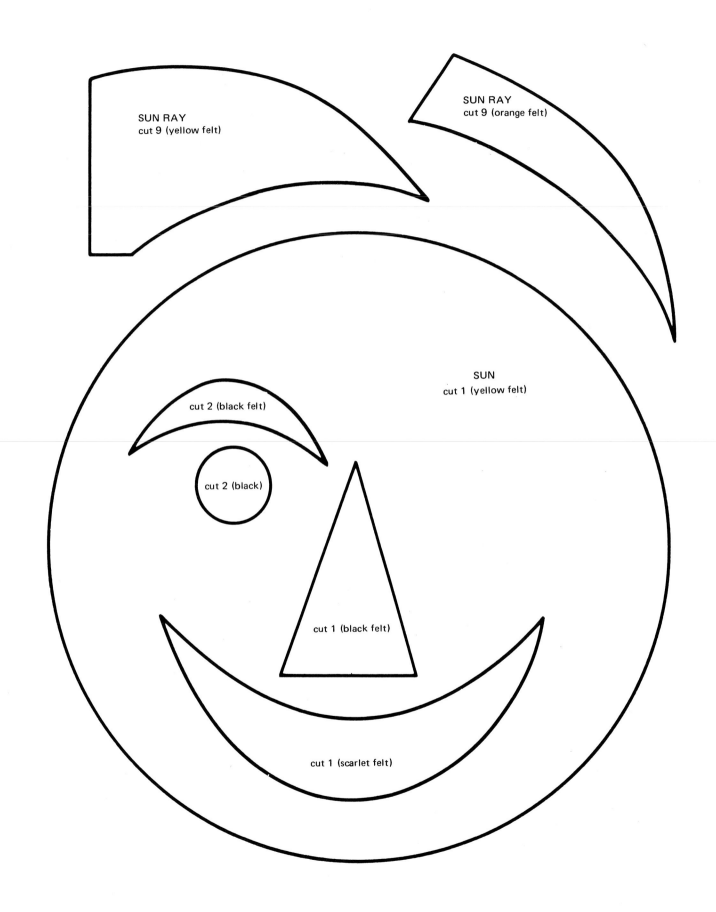

SUN RAY
cut 9 (yellow felt)

SUN RAY
cut 9 (orange felt)

SUN
cut 1 (yellow felt)

cut 2 (black felt)

cut 2 (black)

cut 1 (black felt)

cut 1 (scarlet felt)

Felt flower belt
illustrated in colour on pages 56 and 57

MATERIALS
¼ yd. felt, 36 in. wide, plus small squares or scraps of felt in assorted colours for the flowers and leaves (our belt is made in blue, with flowers and leaves in pink, orange, purple, yellow, blue and green). ¼ yd. mediumweight interfacing, 32 or 36 in. wide. Stranded embroidery cotton to match flower centres.

MEASUREMENTS
Belt can be made to fit any size waist; width of finished belt is approximately 3 in.

TO MAKE
Cut a 1½-in. wide strip of interfacing to length of waist measurement plus 2 in. for ease of fit. Cut a strip of blue felt to the same length but 3¼ in. wide. Pin interfacing along centre of felt, then turn the felt over interfacing along both long edges. Overlap felt edges by ¼ in. and sew firmly in position.

The diagrams below give the templates you will need in actual size: two different flower shapes, leaf shape, and two sizes of circle for flower centres. Using these shapes as a guide, construct your own templates from stiff card.

Using your templates, cut out the shapes from assorted colours of felt. The number of flowers required will depend on the length of the belt. Each flower should have two leaves and a big circle and a little circle (in contrasting colours) cut to go with it.

Position a flower at either end of the felt band, on right side. Space remaining flowers and leaves evenly along the belt. To stitch each motif in position, begin by sewing base of each leaf with small over stitches to the felt band, then position a flower on top, covering the base of the leaves. Place a big circle exactly on centre of the flower shape, and a small circle exactly on the centre of this, then sew these three layers in position together, using three strands of embroidery cotton. Work a cross stitch exactly on centre of small circle, taking stitching right through all layers to felt band behind. Then work five small over stitches, spaced evenly round edge of big circle, and stitching only through this circle and flower shape itself. Stitch all motifs in place in this way.

TO COMPLETE
To make tie strings, cut two lengths of blue felt, each 26 in. by 1 in. Fold long edges of each strip together and stitch, leaving ¾ in. unsewn at one end. Flatten unsewn end of string, and stitch in position one to each end of belt, under the first flower.

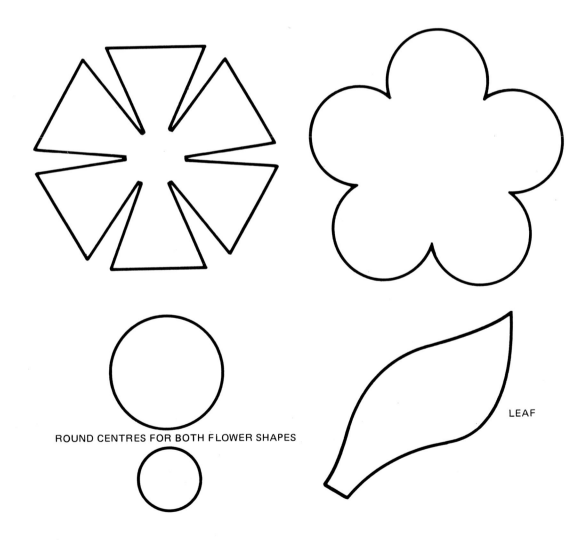

ROUND CENTRES FOR BOTH FLOWER SHAPES

LEAF

Chapter eight
QUILTING

18th-century sample of quilting on linen. The traditional scale pattern forms the background, and the border is mainly in various arrangements of feather patterns.

Quilting is a decorative needlework which developed from a simple basic need to create a warm fabric: a layer of wool or cotton wadding was placed in between two layers of a suitable material. The stitching which held this 'sandwich' together had no more purpose originally than to prevent the filling from moving about. Then it was realised that as well as being practical, the stitching might just as well be decorative too, and so the many beautiful traditional quilting patterns were invented.

One usually thinks of quilting as a form of bedcovering – the word counterpane is derived from *contre-poinct,* a corruption of the French word for back stitch, or quilting stitch as it was also called – and perhaps for bedjackets and dressing-gowns. But the technique can equally effectively be used for attractive, heat-retaining tea and coffee cosies, for children's jackets and coats, for skirts, and all sorts of fashion accessories.

Traditionally, quilting used to be done in white upon a colour, or in one colour upon white. Yellow silk stitching on white was a favourite combination, and gave a beautifully fine and delicate effect. The coloured silk thread as well as creating a design in the stitching gave a tint to the fabric. The Persians produced elaborate

quilting on fine white linen, also sewn with a yellow silk. But the pattern was stuffed with cords of blue cotton, so that the unstitched areas had a fragile bluish tinge, while the areas around the stitching were creamy white from the yellow silk. Today of course, quilting can be worked in any colour, upon almost any fabric, although in general the paler shades work better, for these reflect more light and therefore the stitched pattern will stand out better.

MATERIALS

If you are making an item in which both back and front will be seen then a similar 'outer' fabric should be used for both sides, but if the item is likely to be seen on the one side only, then inexpensive fabric can be used for the underside, provided it is similar in weight to the top fabric. Suitable fabrics for the top layer are satin, silk, dull satin crêpe-de-chine, and man-made fabrics which have a slightly lustrous quality – never use fabrics which are too shiny. Cotton can be used for the under layer, in a weight similar to the top fabric.

For fillings, a number of good synthetic fillings are available nowadays, or you can use cotton wadding, lamb's wool or cotton wool (the natural variety, not the medicated type sold by chemists). For thinner quilting – for a garment, for instance, where bulk is not required – then a lightweight interfacing fabric can be used. Alternatively, flannel or old, well-washed blankets are suitable.

Strong cotton, silk or synthetic thread (according to the fabric chosen) should be used in a colour to match the fabric. Alternatively, if you want the stitching to stand out, then use thread in a contrasting colour to the fabric. This, however, is not generally recommended: the design is created by the puffed-up unstitched areas of fabric – if stitching is eyecatching too the result can be confusing.

YOU ALSO NEED

Good-quality rustless pins – alternatively, needles are often used instead of pins as they never leave marks in even the most delicate fabrics; basting thread; a large darning needle, chalk pencil or dressmaker's tracing paper for transferring designs; two pairs of scissors, one for cutting fabrics, one for cutting threads; templates (see below); a frame – ideally a proper quilting frame should be used, but if you do not want to go to the expense of buying one, or the trouble of making one, then an ordinary, embroidery frame can be used, including the Swiss or tambour frame for small pieces of work. It is possible to work small items in the hand with care, but results are rarely as satisfactory as if the fabrics are held properly stretched and taut throughout working. If you are quilting by machine then, obviously, it will not be possible to use a frame.

PLANNING A DESIGN

The first step in any quilting project is to plan your design. This is marked out on the right side of the upper layer of fabric, and the ideal method to use is to mark out the pattern with the tip of a darning needle – this will leave a faint crease line on the fabric which can be used as a stitching guide.

Alternatively, the design can be marked out in chalk – or perhaps key points, such as the centre and the mid-points of each side, marked in chalk, with the rest needle-marked. Dressmaker's carbon paper can also be used provided you are certain the lines of the marking will be completely covered by stitching when the design is complete.

'Plain' quilting consists simply of even, regular lines across the entire area of work, thus forming diamonds, squares, or sometimes octagons. Such patterns are often known as backgrounds or fillings, and can be used as border patterns for a big design, with a more decorative pattern motif in the centre.

A bedcover, for example, will frequently have an interesting centre pattern motif, designed to fill most of the area which lies on top of the bed; a background or filling pattern is then used for the borders, with perhaps small ornamental motifs filling in the corners if necessary.

There are many attractive traditional patterns for both main patterns and backgrounds and a few are shown on page 135. Once you have discovered how enjoyable quilting can be, you will no doubt go on to create your own designs. Many of the traditional patterns are based on leaf shapes, or are variations on circles or stars. If you study examples of quilting in museums, you will see that some incredibly complex designs have been worked in the past. Examples of work from India, for example, show elaborate pictorial scenes of the chase, battles and ships in full sail. For your first efforts at quilting, it might be better to try something simpler!

The important thing to remember when planning a quilting design, and combining several different pattern motifs, is that the pattern should fill the entire area of fabric. Also, the primary purpose of quilting is to hold the filling securely in place – you should never therefore have unquilted areas of more than about two square inches, otherwise the filling will tend to get displaced.

It is also important to spend time marking out your design accurately – little is worse than an uneven or non-symmetrical quilting pattern. As the edges of your fabric may not necessarily be straight, the first point to establish is the central point then measure out from this, taking care to keep straight lines even. If you use a diamond patterning as a background, and this is interrupted in the centre by a decorative pattern motif, then make sure that the diagonals on one side of the work match up with those on the other.

TEMPLATES

As with patchwork, these are an essential aid to uniform and accurate patterns. Various quilting templates are manufactured in metal and plastic and should be available from any good needlecraft supply shop. But it is perfectly easy to construct your own set of templates from stiff card. As you are likely to want a fair number of different pattern shapes, it is probably a good idea to buy one or two basic shapes, such as circle, diamond, star and rose motifs, then construct a number of others yourself.

In most cases the template gives a basic outline, which can be varied by using different arrangements of stitching lines inside the shape.

A pair of heart motifs.

One small template can often be used to create a larger motif – for instance, the small motif shown above can be used to build up various forms of the traditional feather pattern. Several traditional template shapes are shown on the opposite page.

SEWING YOUR FABRIC

Once your design is clearly and accurately marked out, the next step is to combine the three-layered 'sandwich': the top fabric, the padding and the under fabric or lining. Pin the three layers carefully in position, and baste together – it is important, especially if you are not using a frame, that basting is done firmly and thoroughly. Begin by machine stitching right round outer edges so the layers will not move during stitching, then hand or machine baste across work, horizontally, vertically and diagonally so the entire surface of the work is well covered with lines of basting.

A choice of three stitches is available for the stitching of the design: chain, back or running. Chain stitch is rarely used nowadays, although the effect of working a design from the back in chain stitch can be most attractive.

Running stitch is reasonably quick and easy to do, but it is important to keep stitches and spaces absolutely uniform in length. Back stitch is by the far the firmest stitch as it forms an unbroken outline along the line of the design. If, for instance, you are using an ironed-on transfer design, then you must use back stitch if you are to cover all lines of the transfer. Whichever stitch you choose you must keep to this same stitch throughout the design.

Begin stitching in the centre of your design and gradually work outwards. If you try to work from the top down your fabric will be inclined to pucker or pull out of shape. Work each stitch individually with a positive stabbing movement to make sure stitches go through all three layers of fabric, and remain regular throughout.

If you have a quilting attachment on your sewing machine then stitching can be done by machine – follow the instructions in your machine manual.

FINISHING METHODS

When your design is completely stitched, remove all basting threads. Edges can now be neatened either by turning in the raw edges of outer and under layers and slipstitching them together, or the edges can be encased in seam binding or bias strips of matching fabric. If wished, a cord can be enclosed in the binding to give a firm outer edge – this is popular for bedcovers.

If you intend to stitch two or more pieces of quilted fabric together – to make a jacket or skirt, for instance – then leave fairly wide unquilted edges on the separate pieces. Stitch together in the usual way, using these unquilted edges as turnings. Trim away any excess padding in the turnings. If any of the lines of the quilting design do not go far enough into the seams then add a few more stitches to them.

ITALIAN QUILTING

This form of quilting, which is also sometimes known as corded quilting, is worked with only two layers of fabric, and no filling. The design is stitched in double outline, and then a thick cord or length of thick wool is threaded through this double outline so the design stands out in relief.

Work quilting from the wrong side, then cut a small hole in one channel of the design. Thread cord or wool on to a large blunt-pointed needle and carefully take this through the channel. Be careful not to catch the fabric in as you thread. Rug wool makes a good padding, or several thicknesses of tapestry wool; cotton cord is also suitable. Whichever type of cord or yarn you choose, it is important that it gives a good round padding to your design.

Although cord or wool should normally be chosen to match the fabric colour, an interesting effect can be achieved by using a contrasting colour of cord – with delicate fabrics in particular, the contrast colour will just shine faintly through the corded areas giving a new dimension to your design.

At corners of the design bring needle and cord out to the surface (on the wrong side), allow cord to form a small loop, then take it back into the next channel (see diagram below).

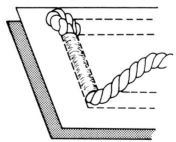

TRAPUNTO QUILTING

This, like Italian quilting, is worked with only two layers of fabric, but in this technique areas of the design are stitched with a single line of stitching, and then these areas are padded with a suitable wadding or filling.

QUILTING PATTERNS

All these patterns can be used in different groupings, and with different stitching arrangements within each motif. Each drawing shows the template outline in solid line; the dotted lines indicate suggested arrangements for stitching.

Rose – showing two different fillings.

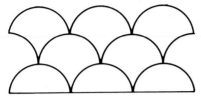

The scale – similar to the scale pattern used in patchwork.

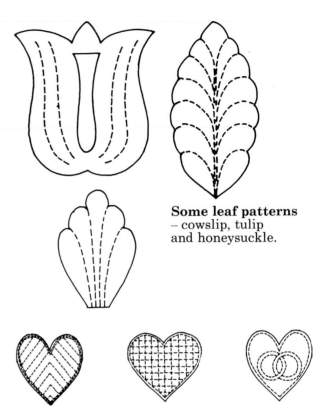

Some leaf patterns – cowslip, tulip and honeysuckle.

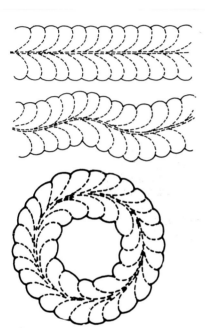

Feather – used in groups to build up complete feather patterns. Straight feather; running feather; feather circle.

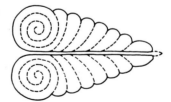

Heart – showing different fillings.

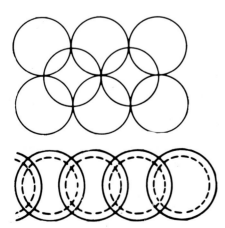

Wine glass – showing different arrangements and fillings.

Scissors – the same template used twice, the second time in reverse, to give a pair of scissors.

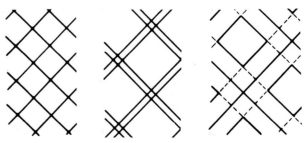

Some background fillings – square diamonds, double diamonds, Victoria diamonds.

135

THE PATTERNS

Quilted cape

MATERIALS
1¾ yd. patterned cotton (or similar fabric), 36 in. wide. 3 yd. matching or toning plain cotton fabric, 36 in. wide. 1¾ yd. Courtelle wadding (or similar synthetic wadding). 6 yd. bias binding to match plain fabric, ½ in. wide. Two buttons, each with a diameter of ⅞ in.

MEASUREMENTS
As cape is loose-fitting, it should comfortably fit bust size 34–38 in.; length at centre back 23 in.

TO MAKE YOUR PATTERN
The diagram opposite gives the pattern pieces you need for the cape: one square on the diagram equals 1 in. Mark out a large sheet of strong brown or white paper into 1-in. squares, then copy the pattern pieces as given on the miniature diagram on to your full-size grid. Each of the squares on the miniature diagram represents one square on your paper. Copy the outlines and positions of lines, curves and angles in relation to the squares as accurately as possible. Cut out the three pattern pieces.

TO MAKE
Using your paper pattern, cut out one main cape section each from patterned fabric, plain fabric, and wadding. In

each case cut from double thickness fabric or wadding, and be sure to place pattern on fold of fabric as indicated on pattern diagram. Cut border section eight times from plain fabric, four times from wadding. Cut collar section twice from double thickness plain fabric, once from double thickness wadding, placing pattern on fold.

Mark entire surface of patterned fabric main cape section with diagonal lines, 1 in. apart, to form diamond quilting. Sandwich wadding shape for main cape section between corresponding plain and patterned fabric sections. Baste fabrics and wadding firmly together, then work quilting.

Join shoulder darts as marked on pattern diagram, right sides of fabric (patterned side) together. Begin stitching dart $\frac{1}{2}$ in. from fabric edge at neck edge then gradually taper stitching to nothing at point of dart. Join four border sections of plain fabric together, with $\frac{1}{2}$ in. seams, to form one side of cape lower edging. Repeat with other four border sections to make other side of edging. On right side of one border section, mark the dotted border lines, as shown in pattern diagram.

The diagram below gives the heart template in actual size. Using this as a guide, construct your own template from stiff card. Using this template, mark out the heart pattern all along the fabric, within the border lines already marked. Begin with a heart pointing inwards 2$\frac{1}{2}$ in. from each end of border, then space pairs of hearts between. Sandwich wadding between plain fabric shapes. Baste thoroughly, then work quilting.

On right side of one collar fabric section, mark out a heart motif pointing inwards at either end of the collar, and then mark three pairs of hearts between. Sandwich wadding between the two fabric shapes, and baste thoroughly. Work quilting.

TO COMPLETE

Turn in $\frac{1}{2}$ in. along bottom edge of main cape section. Lay this edge over right side of border section so that it just overlaps without covering row of border stitching. Stitch neatly together. Turn in neck edge of cape main section for $\frac{1}{2}$ in. Place this edge over wrong side of neck edge of collar, so it just overlaps, and sew together. Neaten inside of seam. Bind front opening edges, lower edge and edges of collar with bias binding.

Stitch one button to each side of cape at neck, and make a rouleau loop to fasten.

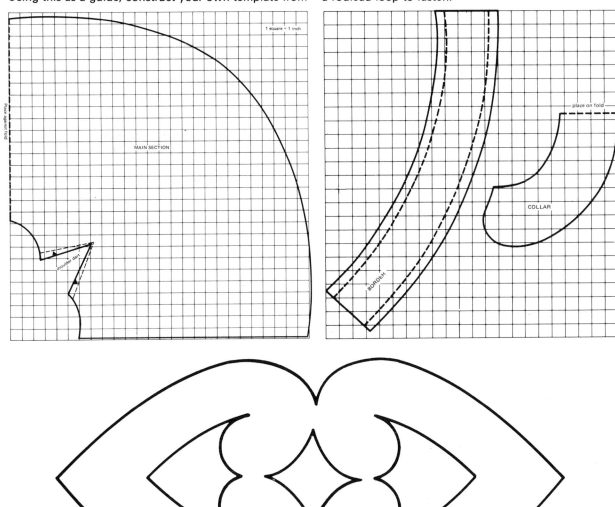

HEART TEMPLATE (actual size)

Child's reversible jacket

illustrated in colour on page 124

MATERIALS

$\frac{7}{8}$ yd. soft wool fabric, 36 in. wide, in first colour (red), and $\frac{7}{8}$ yd. of a similar fabric in second colour (blue). $\frac{7}{8}$ yd. Courtelle wadding (or similar synthetic wadding). One packet bias binding tape, $\frac{1}{2}$ in. wide, to match one of fabrics.

MEASUREMENTS

The jacket is fairly loose-fitting, so should comfortably fit chest size 26–28 in.; length at centre back 16 in.

TO MAKE YOUR PATTERN

The diagram, right, gives the pattern pieces you will need for the jacket: one square on the diagram equals 1 in. Mark out a large sheet of strong brown or white paper into 1-in. squares, then copy the pattern pieces as given in the miniature diagram on to your full-size grid. Each of the squares on the miniature diagram represents one square on your paper. Copy the outlines and positions of lines, curves and angles in relation to the squares as accurately as possible. Cut out the two pattern pieces.

TO MAKE

Using your paper pattern, cut out jacket back and front pieces from both fabrics, and from the Courtelle wadding. In every case cut from double thickness fabric or wadding, placing centre back of back section to fold of fabric, as indicated on diagram.

The feather template is given below in actual size. Using this as a guide, make your own template in stiff card. Mark a vertical row of feathering down centre front opening of jacket on left and right fronts. Begin at lower edge and mark in first feather motif, then place template immediately above this first motif, so lower line of template fits exactly on top line of first motif, and with straight edge still lining up with front edges of jacket. Mark in motif, and continue in this way. At neckline edge of jacket, use only enough of the motif to fill space available. The rest of the jacket will be quilted with lines of vertical stitching, spaced $\frac{3}{4}$ in. apart. Carefully mark lines over remaining surface of fronts and back, beginning first line on fronts $\frac{1}{8}$ in. from feathering, and then spacing other lines at $\frac{3}{4}$-in. intervals.

Sandwich wadding between corresponding shapes of fabric, having one layer in first colour, and one in second. Baste firmly together (see page 134), then work quilting either by machine (see note below), or with firm back stitches. Leave $\frac{1}{2}$ in. unstitched at shoulder and side edges.

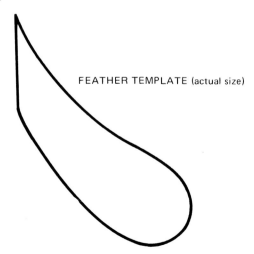

FEATHER TEMPLATE (actual size)

TO COMPLETE

Place jacket fronts and back together, with red sides facing. With $\frac{1}{2}$-in. turnings, stitch shoulder and side seams, only stitching red fabric. Trim turnings, and trim away wadding from seams. Turn in $\frac{1}{2}$-in. seam allowances on sides and shoulders on blue fabric, and slipstitch neatly. Make stitches as small and invisible as possible. Bind armholes, neck, centre front opening and lower edge of jacket with bias binding.

Note. This design was quilted by machine, with blue thread used in the sewing machine spool for underneath stitching, and scarlet thread for the top stitching, to match the two fabric colours used.

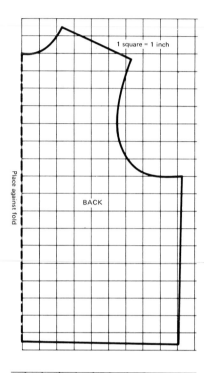

1 square = 1 inch

Place against fold

BACK

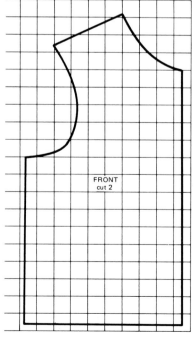

FRONT
cut 2

Wine-glass patterned muff

MATERIALS
$\frac{3}{4}$ yd. satin-back crêpe fabric (or similar suitable fabric), 36 in. wide. $\frac{3}{4}$ yd. Courtelle (or similar synthetic wadding). Thin cotton fabric, 14 in. by 22 in., to match crêpe fabric. $1\frac{1}{2}$ yd. twisted cord to match crêpe fabric.

MEASUREMENTS
Finished muff measures approximately $10\frac{1}{2}$ in. long by 9 in. deep.

TO MAKE
From crêpe fabric, cut two shapes, each 14 in. by 22 in. From wadding, cut one shape, 14 in. by 22 in., and two shapes, each $10\frac{3}{4}$ in. by 20 in. From the cotton fabric cut one shape, 14 in. by 22 in.
Place one of the crêpe fabric shapes, right side up, on a flat board or similar clean, flat surface. Stretching it as tautly as possible pin it to the board, or use self-adhesive tape to hold it in place. Now using the base of a wine glass with a diameter of about 2 in., or a circular cardboard template, mark out the wine glass pattern all over fabric (see page 135). It is easier to use a glass rather than a card template, as it is then possible to see through the glass and check that the overlapping pattern being formed is regular.
Remove fabric from board, and place on top of wadding of the same size, then place wadding on top of the thin cotton fabric shape. Baste thoroughly together, then work quilting.
Place quilted fabric on top of the two remaining wadding shapes, and trim to the same size. Baste together.
Turn back the satin side of crêpe along the two long sides of shape to make a satin border $\frac{5}{8}$ in. wide. Stitch. Place short ends of shape together, right sides facing, and stitch with $\frac{1}{2}$-in. turnings. Slipstitch seams flat.
Use the second crêpe fabric shape to line the muff, using the satin side of fabric as right side. Turn in edges of fabric to fit muff, and slipstitch neatly in place.
Turn muff right side out. Loop twisted cord through muff. Attach ends of cord firmly inside.

139

Scale-patterned collar and cuffs

MATERIALS

$\frac{3}{4}$ yd. thin cotton fabric (alternatively, silk or satin could could be used), 36 in. wide. $\frac{1}{2}$ yd. Courtelle wadding (or similar synthetic wadding). Bias binding, $\frac{1}{2}$ in. wide, to match fabric.

MEASUREMENTS

Collar: approximately 26 in. long, $5\frac{3}{4}$ in. deep. **Cuffs:** approximately $10\frac{1}{2}$ in. long, $4\frac{1}{2}$ in. deep.

TO MAKE YOUR PATTERN

The diagram opposite gives the pattern pieces you will need for the collar and cuffs: one square on the diagram equals 1 in. Mark out a sheet of strong brown or white paper into 1-in. squares, then copy the pattern pieces as given in the miniature diagram on to your full-size grid. Each of the squares on the miniature diagram represents one square on your paper. Copy the outlines and positions of lines, curves and angles in relation to the squares as accurately as possible. Cut out the two pattern pieces.

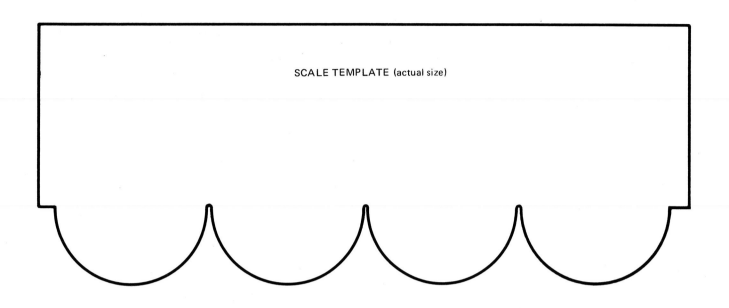

SCALE TEMPLATE (actual size)

TO MAKE

Using your paper pattern, cut out four cuff shapes, and two collar shapes from the fabric. Cut two cuff shapes and one collar shape from wadding.

The scale template is given above in actual size. Using this as a guide, make your own template in stiff card. Mark out entire surface of one collar section and two cuffs in scale pattern, arranging the rows so the curve of each scale fits between two curves of previous row to give a neat, interlocking arrangement.

Sandwich wadding between corresponding marked and unmarked fabric shapes. Baste firmly together (see page 134).

Work quilting with firm back stitches.

TO COMPLETE

Bind outside edges of collar and cuffs with bias binding. Bind inside edges with two lengths of bias binding to give a wider edging for attaching collar and cuffs to garments.

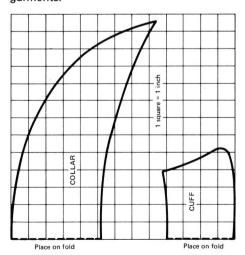

1 square = 1 inch

COLLAR

CUFF

Place on fold   Place on fold

Italian quilted evening bag

illustrated in colour on page 125

MATERIALS

Piece of satin, $10\frac{1}{4}$ in. by $22\frac{1}{2}$ in. Piece of lining fabric $10\frac{1}{4}$ in. by $22\frac{1}{2}$ in., to match or contrast with satin. Piece of mediumweight interfacing, $10\frac{1}{4}$ in. by $22\frac{1}{2}$ in. Piece of lightweight, firmly-woven fabric, 10 in. by $8\frac{1}{2}$ in., for backing the quilting. 2 yd. rug wool or soft cotton cord to match satin. $\frac{1}{2}$ yd. narrow gold chain for bag handle. One large press fastener.

MEASUREMENTS

Finished bag, excluding handle, measures 9 in. by approximately $7\frac{1}{4}$ in.

TO MAKE

The diagram on page 142 gives the motif in actual size. Place satin fabric right side up on a flat surface, so long edges are at the sides. Trace the motif centrally on to satin 1 in. up from lower edge of fabric.

Place the backing fabric centrally on to wrong side of traced pattern, and baste in position. Stitch along lines of pattern, then thread rug wool or cotton cord between the lines of the design (see page 134), to create a raised quilted pattern.

Baste quilted fabric to interfacing, wrong sides together. Measure $7\frac{1}{4}$ in. from unquilted end of fabric and fold fabric on this line, right sides together. Stitch side seams, with $\frac{1}{2}$-in. turnings. This makes the pocket of the bag; the remaining quilted section will fold over the pocket to become the bag flap. Turn bag right side out. Turn in seam allowance on flap edges and baste.

Make up lining to fit bag. Insert into bag, wrong sides together, and slipstitch in place.

TO COMPLETE

Stitch one end of chain to each side of bag at top of pocket, under flap. Sew press fastener to fasten centre of bottom edge of flap to pocket.

TOP EDGE

SIDE EDGE

MOTIF IN ACTUAL SIZE

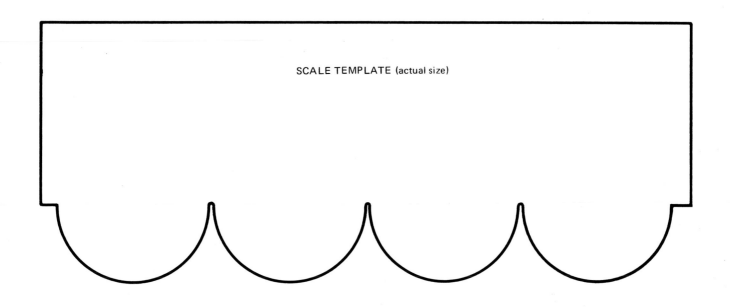

SCALE TEMPLATE (actual size)

TO MAKE

Using your paper pattern, cut out four cuff shapes, and two collar shapes from the fabric. Cut two cuff shapes and one collar shape from wadding.

The scale template is given above in actual size. Using this as a guide, make your own template in stiff card. Mark out entire surface of one collar section and two cuffs in scale pattern, arranging the rows so the curve of each scale fits between two curves of previous row to give a neat, interlocking arrangement.

Sandwich wadding between corresponding marked and unmarked fabric shapes. Baste firmly together (see page 134).

Work quilting with firm back stitches.

TO COMPLETE

Bind outside edges of collar and cuffs with bias binding. Bind inside edges with two lengths of bias binding to give a wider edging for attaching collar and cuffs to garments.

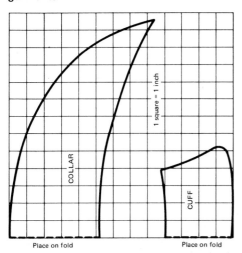

1 square = 1 inch

COLLAR

CUFF

Place on fold   Place on fold

Italian quilted evening bag

illustrated in colour on page 125

MATERIALS

Piece of satin, 10¼ in. by 22½ in. Piece of lining fabric 10¼ in. by 22½ in., to match or contrast with satin. Piece of mediumweight interfacing, 10¼ in. by 22½ in. Piece of lightweight, firmly-woven fabric, 10 in. by 8½ in., for backing the quilting. 2 yd. rug wool or soft cotton cord to match satin. ½ yd. narrow gold chain for bag handle. One large press fastener.

MEASUREMENTS

Finished bag, excluding handle, measures 9 in. by approximately 7¼ in.

TO MAKE

The diagram on page 142 gives the motif in actual size. Place satin fabric right side up on a flat surface, so long edges are at the sides. Trace the motif centrally on to satin 1 in. up from lower edge of fabric.

Place the backing fabric centrally on to wrong side of traced pattern, and baste in position. Stitch along lines of pattern, then thread rug wool or cotton cord between the lines of the design (see page 134), to create a raised quilted pattern.

Baste quilted fabric to interfacing, wrong sides together. Measure 7¼ in. from unquilted end of fabric and fold fabric on this line, right sides together. Stitch side seams, with ½-in. turnings. This makes the pocket of the bag; the remaining quilted section will fold over the pocket to become the bag flap. Turn bag right side out. Turn in seam allowance on flap edges and baste.

Make up lining to fit bag. Insert into bag, wrong sides together, and slipstitch in place.

TO COMPLETE

Stitch one end of chain to each side of bag at top of pocket, under flap. Sew press fastener to fasten centre of bottom edge of flap to pocket.

TOP EDGE

SIDE EDGE

MOTIF IN ACTUAL SIZE

142

Finishing touches

WASHING YOUR EMBROIDERIES

Most embroideries, worked on good-quality fabric with good-quality threads, may be safely washed in warm water and soap powder. Always squeeze the article in the soapy water very gently. Rinse thoroughly in warm water, squeeze by hand and leave until half dry. Iron on wrong side when still slightly damp.

To give a light stiffening to fine work, wet a piece of new organdie, and place this over the wrong side of the embroidery. Press over it until the organdie is completely dry. The finishing starch in the organdie will then be transferred to the embroidery and give it a slight stiffening.

Embroideries should in fact be pressed in the course of working as well as when you have finished a design. Damp thoroughly and place the work face downwards on top of a thick pad of fabric so threads will not be crushed. Choose iron setting to suit the fabric, and press well.

Coloured embroideries

If the colourfast qualities of either fabric or threads are not known, then great care should be taken when laundering coloured work. Never pile coloured embroideries on top of each other, or fold over on themselves. The best way to dry a coloured embroidery is to lay it flat between two dry clean cloths, then roll it up. Faded colours can be revived by adding a little white vinegar to the final rinsing water.

Canvas embroideries

A piece of embroidery worked on canvas must always be dry cleaned as the use of water would soften the canvas.

MAKING-UP HINTS

Cushions

Cut fabric into two equal pieces, then complete embroidery on one piece. Place fabrics right sides together and machine stitch three sides, leaving the fourth side open to allow the cushion pad or filling to be inserted easily. Press seams and turn to right side. Insert pad or filling. Turn in the seam allowance on the open edges and slipstitch neatly together.

Pictures

Place the embroidery centrally over cardboard cut to a suitable size, fold the surplus fabric to the back and secure at the top with pins into edge of cardboard. Pull firmly over the lower edge and pin in position. Repeat on side edges, pulling fabric until it lies taut on the cardboard. Secure at the back by lacing from side to side, vertically and horizontally, with strong thread. Remove pins. The picture may then be mounted and framed if wished.

Mitred corners

A mitre is a fold used to achieve smooth shaping at a corner. To mitre a corner of a hem, fold and press the hem; open out the hem and fold the corner inwards on the inner fold line. Cut off the corner, leaving a small seam allowance (diagram A). Refold the hem and slipstitch the diagonal line of the mitre in position (diagram B).

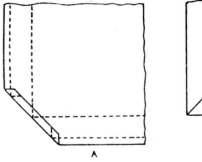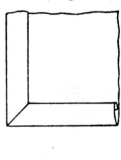

A   B

Taped edges

Facing hem edges with bias binding gives a neat, flat finish to such items as tablecloths, mats, runners and so on. To apply the bias binding, first open one fold of the binding tape, and lay on fabric edge to edge, right sides together. Machine stitch along the fold mark of binding. Turn binding over to wrong side of fabric and stitch invisibly to fabric along the fold edge of binding. For binding, a $\frac{1}{4}$-in. seam allowance beyond the finished size is sufficient.

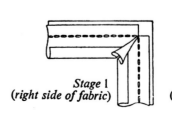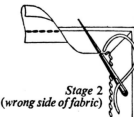

Stage 1
(right side of fabric)   *Stage 2*
                        (wrong side of fabric)

Acknowledgements

The author acknowledges with thanks the help given with the preparation of this book by the following:

J. & P. Coats Ltd., 155 St. Vincent Street, Glasgow C.2.
Victoria and Albert Museum, London—for permission to reproduce photographs on pages 40 and 132. Both are Crown copyright.
Barbara Snook—for samples and designs illustrated on pages 8, 12, 13, 16, 20, 42, 43, 45, 46, 50, 64 (two canvas work samplers), 67, 68, 70, 71, 83, 86, 88, 89, 106, 118, and 125 (the Florentine and drawn-thread cushion cover).
Kate Pountney—for patchwork, appliqué and quilting designs illustrated on pages 56, 57, 104, 108, 113, 117, 120, 121, 123, 124, 125, 128, 136, 139 and 140.
Joan Lodge—for samples and designs illustrated on pages 11, 56 and 57 (canvas work belt), 60, 64 (duck panel), 69, 79, 86, 93, 107, 114, 115 and 119.
Mrs. F. M. Blake—for smocking samples illustrated on pages 84 and 85.

USA equivalents

Needle sizes and thread qualities in the USA are generally similar to those used in the United Kingdom. There are also good-quality multi-purpose threads available both in the UK and the USA which can be used with most fabrics and for most purposes. If Clark's Anchor Stranded Cotton is not readily available, then J. & P. Coats Deluxe Six Strand Floss can be substituted, and will give satisfactory results. The colour range is wide, and there should be an equivalent shade for each shade of Anchor Stranded Cotton. If Coats Anchor Tapisserie Wool is not readily available, then any good-quality tapestry wool can be satisfactorily substituted.